Sociological Perspectives in Education

SOCIOLOGICAL PERSPECTIVES IN EDUCATION

Models for Analysis

JACK L. NELSON
RUTGERS UNIVERSITY
& FRANK P. BESAG
UNIVERSITY OF WASHINGTON

PITMAN PUBLISHING CORPORATION
New York Toronto London Tel Aviv

Library of Congress Catalog Card Number: 74-94650
Manufactured in the United States of America
DESIGNED BY VINCENT TORRE
1.987654321

Contents

PART III

THE SCHOOL IN SOCIAL PERSPECTIVE

Preface

Several blind men touched different portions of the same elephant. Each described the elephant differently, having filtered his experience through his own perspective. The shape, purpose, size, and interrelatedness of the elephant's parts, as described by these blind men, were unrecognizable by anyone seeing the entire animal. Who has the truer knowledge? One could argue that those with eyesight have no more accurate knowledge of an elephant than the blind men because the perceptions of each rely on different senses and different frameworks.

The observer of a society and its schools must also rely on a variety of perceptions in understanding the complexities of the system. Through communication he can also utilize the senses of other observers. Nevertheless, the dimensions of a society and its institutions make it impossible for him to obtain a total view; like the man in front of the elephant, he is limited by his perceptions. He can only strive to fit together the segments in a number of ways, making use of his own "filtering screen," his perspective, and his perceptions.

This book offers both a choice of filtration agents and observations—the knowledge of education and society which has resulted from research—of other men. The analytic models offered here are drawn from theories of social institutions, while the information sections are representative of available knowledge relevant to the study of schools in a society.

Two basic purposes of this book are to stimulate interest in the study of education from sociological perspectives and to encourage the refinement of analytic methods and data. Theories concerning sociology and education need continual investigation and revision. Even "certain" knowledge demands questioning.

The story of the blind men and the elephant has the defects of any moralistic writing, but though analogies are seldom perfect, they may still be insightful. Although a society and its schools are elephantine phenomena and observers are sightless in many respects, an increased understanding of the nature and processes of education may be beneficial to both observers and practitioners.

This brings us to the nature of this book. A description and analysis of the field of sociology and its relation to education is presented first as a means of providing a framework within which the schools can be perceived. Agreement and dissent in sociology and education, discussed in Part I, suggests a variety of potential models for analysis of the schools.

Four main analytic models are selected for explication and application to schools as social institutions in Part II. Each model has distinct qualities which can be used in understanding education in sociological terms. They differ in form, method, and interpretation, but not in purpose. These models are adaptations of sociological theory for use in analyzing education. Their purpose is to provide methods for understanding schools; and the rationale for providing several in this treatise is to encourage both understanding of the institution and consideration of a variety of means of sociological analysis. This wedding of theory and practice is important because of the continual need to develop and improve theory, and the necessity of testing theory in the caldron of practice. However, the utopian aspects of this approach are recognized.

Sociological and educational theory are both dynamic; no absolute truths are self-evident. This makes the testing of theory very difficult, but it should enhance the opportunity to improve theory by rejecting portions of it which do not match accepted truth at any point in time. At the other end of the theory-practice continuum, teachers, administrators, parents, school boards, and students must make key decisions about the operation of schools, and they cannot wait for consistent theory to evolve. Thus imperfect theory, imperfect models, and imperfect applications are assumed, but not approved. The models used herein are not, of course, the only models available, and they suffer from imperfections in their theoretical base or application, but they constitute viable ways of analyzing schools and offer opportunity for improving the models or their application.

Part III provides an example of the macrosociology of education by using gross data and interpretation of education in the social order. Its purpose is to sketch the structure and function of education and some essential characteristics of social structure in America. This section is a relatively global approach to school and society which has both a value and a data base. The values and data are mutually supportive.

Part IV is composed of treatments of specific topics regarding the nature of schools and students. While Part III deals largely with external influences on education and is concerned with broad social and school norms, Part IV illustrates topics related to the impact of schools as socialization agencies upon atypical groups within the schools. It is a view of internal influences within schools and of those students who deviate from the norms and values of school and society. Atypical groups were selected for treatment because they provide more dramatic illustration of the school in its socialization role within the social context. Social and school control, deviant behavior, and the interaction among them are easier to observe in the more extreme cases.

Parts I and III (with the exception of Chapter 11) were prepared by Jack Nelson; Parts II and IV and Chapter 11 by Frank Besag. The book has been constructed to show dimensions of sociology useful in analyzing education, to offer models for analysis, and to provide large- and small-scale interpretations of schools in society. It is not intended to be a comprehensive survey covering all possible fields and topics. Rather it is intended to stimulate inquiry into the nature and operation of schools.

JACK L. NELSON
FRANK P. BESAG

PART I

SOCIOLOGY AND EDUCATION

Written language is a human phenomenon. As a means of communication it has both advantages and faults. One advantage is its reproducibility and consequent availability for wide and lasting dissemination. One fault is its abstractness and resulting susceptibility for lack of clarity. Dictionaries are printed to assist in defining words (parts of language) by using other words. So long as there is mutual agreement about the concrete meaning of terms, definitions are not a problem. Thus an inch, a pound, or paper can be defined clearly. As the meanings become more abstract, however, the likelihood of disagreement or multiple definitions increases.

Sociology and education are also human phenomena, and both depend upon language. Because the terms sociology and education are abstract and therefore subject to disagreement and multiple definitions, Part I includes a discussion of definitions, viewpoints on the dimensions of sociology, and some ideas about the relationship of sociology to education.

Chapter 1 / *Definitions, Dimensions, and Directions*

Defining Sociology

Although sociologists differ in their definitions of sociology, there is some agreement concerning the basic interests and methods of study. In 1964 Jackson Toby declared that there is no standard definition of sociology, but suggested that the field is concerned with interrelationships among persons and the effect of "societal values on the expression of human motivation."[1] Ten years earlier Ely Chinoy said, "Sociology studies the behavior of human beings in society."[2] Chinoy suggested that the concepts of sociology define the nature and limits of the field. These concepts include culture, society, social groups, function and change, institution, and diffusion.[3] Two basic facts of sociology that Chinoy utilized to analyze social phenomena are that "The behavior of human beings shows regular and recurrent patterns, and human beings are social animals."[4]

Despite the use of differing language, however, sociologists have tended to agree on the broad scope of sociology and the most prominent areas of study within it. The definitions in Table 1 demonstrate this general agreement.

The common thread among these definitions is sociology's attempt to understand social, or group, phenomena. The types of questions asked, hypotheses presented, data sought, conclusions offered, and theories developed by sociologists relate to the interaction of man and society. Thus, the sociologist inquires into the wide variety of human life in groups, seeking to discover both common and deviant patterns of life.

Certainly, other fields, such as anthropology, biology, economics, education, ethnology, geography, history, law, medicine, philosophy, political science, and psychology, also are concerned with group life. This is an argument neither for the uniqueness of the sociological enterprise, nor for the supremacy of its approach to social phenomena. As social scientists and historians have matured in their attempts to comprehend human action and interaction, they have recognized the merits of multiple-field data collection and evaluation. They often borrow both data and methods from related fields. Thus historians are interested in field studies by anthropologists and sociologists; and social psychologists share an interest in decision-making processes in groups with political scientists, philosophers, educationists, and economists. Many social scientists are involved in cross-field studies of group behaviors, either in individual research using data and methodology from another field, or in team efforts representing several fields.

Thus we cannot assume that sociology is preeminent in its application to education. Sociology is a particularly useful and sufficiently broad field for investigating formal and informal education, and it provides a fascinating vantage point for description and analysis of the social phenomena which influence education. It is one of many means for understanding the complex character of education, and its distinction lies in the types of questions and forms of analysis it provides.

For the purposes of this text, let us define sociology simply as *the study of social phenomena.* What then is the accumu-

TABLE 1

Definitions of Sociology

Sociologist	Definition
Talcott Parsons	. . . the science which attempts to develop an analytical theory of social action systems insofar as these systems can be understood in terms of the property common-value integration[a]
Arnold Rose	. . . the science of human relations[b]
Donald Martindale and Elio Monachesi	. . . the discipline that describes the phenomena that are created by the social interaction of human beings and the manner in which these phenomena affect the behavior of individuals[c]
Kurt Wolff	. . . [the discipline which] asks what happens to men and by what rules they behave, not insofar as they unfold their understandable individual existences in their totalities, but insofar as they form groups and are determined by their group existence because of interaction[d]
Alex Inkeles	. . . the study of systems of social action and of their interrelations[e]
Charles H. Page	. . . the study of social relationships, of group-based patterns of behavior, of functional interconnections among social and cultural phenomena, and a holistic conception of the social order[f]
Emile Durkheim	. . . the science of societies[g]
Max Weber	. . . a science which attempts the interpretive understanding of social action in order thereby to arrive at a causal explanation of its course and effects[h]

[a]Talcott Parsons, *The Structure of Social Action*, McGraw-Hill, New York, 1937, p. 768.

[b]Arnold Rose, *Sociology: The Study of Human Relations*, Knopf, New York, 1956, p. 3.

[c]Don Martindale and Elio Monachesi, *Elements of Sociology*, Harper & Row, New York, 1951, p. 39.

[d]Kurt H. Wolff, ed. and trans. *The Sociology of George Simmel*, Free Press, New York, 1950, p. 11.

[e]Alex Inkeles, *What is Sociology*?, Prentice-Hall, Englewood Cliffs, N.J., 1964, p. 16.

[f]Charles H. Page, ed., *Sociology and Contemporary Education*, Random House, New York, 1964, p. 4.

[g]Emile Durkheim, "The Dualism of Human Nature and Its Social Conditions," in Kurt H. Wolff, ed., *Emile Durkheim, 1858–1917*, Ohio State University Press, Columbus, 1960.

[h]Max Weber, A. Henderson and T. Parsons, trans., *Theory of Social and Economic Organization*, Oxford University Press, Fair Lawn, N.J., 1947.

lated content of the field, and what methods are used to study the phenomena related to it?

The Content of Sociology

According to Ely Chinoy, the content of sociology includes several concepts: culture, society, social groups, function and change, institution, and diffusion.[5] W. J. H. Sprott states that, "If we call the actual intention which people have 'first-order data,' then the socially accepted form in which these intentions are satisfied may be called 'second-order data' and it is with *them* that sociology is concerned."[6] Thus the *first-order data*, the original intention of persons (mating by male and female) was to satisfy human needs, but from this intention grew *second-order data*, the establishment of social institutions (marriage, monogamy, polygamy). These second-order social arrangements are abstract conceptions which provide both the basis for socially acceptable behavior and the content for the field of sociology. Chinoy's list of concepts in sociology fits this description. The original intention of man coming together in groups was a result of needs, not a desire to establish culture.

Sprott notes that second-order data become the focus of man's intentions when man becomes cognizant of them. Thus "a nation only exists because appropriate numbers of people believe it exists."[7] Yet, once the abstract conception of *nation* exists, it can become the object of a group's intentions (to establish, expand or even destroy a nation). This modification, which puts social constructs into an active relation with man, expands the content of sociology, for not only would it include study of constructs like family, army, caste, class, gang, city, bureaucracy, population, and education, but also the interrelations among these and their impact on the involved.

Caroline Rose differs somewhat from Sprott in suggesting the content of sociology. She states that "The two main theoretical fields of sociology are Social Organization and Social Psychology."[8] In commenting on social organization, she includes illustrations of institutions, small voluntary groups, and stratified groups. Similar to the modification proposed by

Sprott, she also notes relationships among and within groups and the effects of the environment. Rose offers the following topics as content, in addition to social organization and social psychology: history of sociology, social problems, and demography.[9]

Perhaps the clearest indication of the content of sociology is available in Alex Inkeles' introductory book.[10] He suggests that its content has four basic parts:

1. *Sociological analysis*: the method of sociological inquiry and its application to culture and society
2. *Primary units of social life*: topics from personality to groups to society, and the social character of each
3. *Basic social institutions*: socially structured relations such as family, religion, education, art, welfare, and law
4. *Fundamental social processes*: such areas as social cooperation, conflict, control, change, integration, deviance, and communication

Inkeles' classification of the content of sociology is a convenient means for viewing education as a social phenomenon. Application of sociological analysis to educational structures and functions can be fruitful for educationists and sociologists. Education can be viewed as related to a number of primary units of social life: individual learning, family training, group instruction, and transmission of the accumulated knowledge of a society. Obviously, education is one of the basic social institutions. And the fundamental social processes are in operation and easily observable in an educational environment. These topics are treated in detail in later parts of this book; they illustrate several ways in which sociology offers a great deal to the study of education, and education is a valuable area for sociological investigation. This mutual concern is discussed in the last chapter of this part.

Methods of Sociological Inquiry

The rationale for separating the content of sociology from its methods of study is simply to assist in understanding the processes, tools, and models useful in obtaining, sorting, and evaluating the data from which sociological content is distilled. Of course, the method of study and the nature of sociological content should be consistent and congruent, because the method is influenced by the content and vice versa.

In discussing the methods of study employed in sociology it is important to deal with a current problem in socio-scientific research. The basic conflict concerns the relative worth of passionate study of and active involvement in social problems on the one hand, and dispassionate study, objective evaluation, and empirical presentation of data on the other. This conflict has been given various names: subjective-objective, normative-empirical, and absolutist-relativist. It occurs throughout the social and behavioral sciences, wherever a decision about the treatment of social values determines the method of study and manner of analyzing.

The early sociologists tended toward *deterministic* or single-causation explanations of social phenomena. Auguste Comte, who first named the field *sociology*, proposed a single-channel pattern of development which he called the three phases of history: (1) theological explanations, (2) metaphysical explanations, and (3) positive or scientific explanations (the realm of sociology).[11] This he termed the *General Theory of Human Progress*. Joseph Roucek suggests that nineteenth-century sociologists tried to find a comprehensive theory of society and change. According to Roucek, they "postulated men advancing steadily in time, . . . [envisioning a] linear evolutionism.[12]

The method of study for deterministic sociology was similar to that of moral philosophy: solid belief in the righteousness of a value position, then study of total systems to show the proof. In sociology the movement in social evolution was toward an always improving society. This view has been discounted by recent sociologists, who point out that the state of the contemporary world does not demonstrate straight-line evolution to an improved society.[13] Evolutionism demanded a value commitment which many sociologists today are unwilling to make.

The opposite position to deterministic or moralistic sociology is *scientific* and *mathematical* sociology. The rapid development of statistics and mathematical models since the 1940s has had an important impact on sociological study, indeed the possibility of analyzing data by using devices which require no moral commitment from the social scientist is appealing. The sociologist can remain neutral, collect and quantify data, feed it into a computer for analysis, and then report the findings. This method of study obviates some abstract, nonquantifiable ideas and unobservable social values; but it offers clean, neat tables and charts for social dissection. It also provides a means for relating microcosmic data to macrocosmic phenomena. By proper statistical procedures, theories can be tested on relatively small groups, and conclusions can be drawn which implicate large segments of a society. This has led to what Roucek calls "neo-positivistic empiricism."[14] The result may be a loss of concern for humanity in the press for numbering and counting.

C. Wright Mills criticizes both extremes of sociological study. He believes that ". . . social science as a whole is both intellectually and morally confused. And what is called sociology is very much in the middle of this confusion. . . . [At] the extreme limits of sociological study are those who are aligned with and consider themselves to be of the same cloth as chemists and physicists—and those who align themselves in aim and often method with novelists and even of poets."[15] Mills advocates that sociological thinkers adopt the criteria of the classical tradition by exposing themselves to the writings of the classical sociologists.

Seymour Lipset notes the trend toward a quantitative sociology in an introduction written in 1964 to a book of essays by T. H. Marshall, an English sociologist. Lipset states that sociology has been criticized for forsaking the historical concerns of its nineteenth-century initiators. The shift that Lipset is describing is a change from the macroscopic view of early sociologists to the microscopic analyses of later sociologists: ". . . from studies of social change and aspects of total societies, viewed in a historical and comparative perspective, to the study of interpersonal relations, the structure of small groups, and the analysis of the decision-making process, accompanied by an emphasis on improving the quantitative methodology appropriate to these topics."[16] In this sense the modern sociologist, as Mills suggested, has moved away from the intellectual base of the founders of the field. Lipset, however, goes on to state that the trend reversed itself during the 1960s. He points out that there has been a renaissance of interest in historical and comparative sociology, as exemplified by recent developments in the sociology of science, studies of change in intellectual life, and the present concern for development of national values.[17]

Marvin Bressler comments on three approaches to sociology which he describes as science, action, and significance. Table 2 shows Bressler's conception of the differences among these three ideal types of sociological study.

Bressler notes that the *action* sociologist has a basic set of values (the "American Creed" for American sociologists) and uses his analysis of the disparity between what ought to be (the values) and what is (reality) to move the society to action. His methods of study would include analysis of statistical data, interviews and observations, and comparisons with widely accepted social values. The *significance* sociologist considers grand-scale phenomena of general social concern and attempts to judge major movements and their impact. His methods of study include historical and philosophical analysis, theory building, and hypothesis development. The *science* or *scientific* sociologist attempts to limit social inquiry to those phenomena which can be measured, and continues to refine the instruments of measurement. His methods of study include survey and experimental research, empirical data gathering and analysis, and nonvalue involvement in interpretation.[18]

As a result of the internecine warfare between value-laden and value-free, between humanistic and scientific sociologists, the field of sociology has retained an extremely broad range of opportunity for inquiry into the nature of society. This openness of inquiry is especially valuable for educational study since the field of education has been undergoing a similar transformation in method of study and nature of the field. Value-laden studies which presume the inherent goodness of education or schools have long dominated the study of edu-

TABLE 2

Bressler's Diagram of Salient Characteristics of Three Ideal Types

CHARACTERISTIC	SCIENCE		ACTION	SIGNIFICANCE
	Theory	Empirical Research		
Role Model	Natural scientist		Engineer	European intellectual
Primary Goal	Social knowledge		Solution of social problems	Social criticism
Value Perspective	Ethnic neutrality		Guided by dominant American value orientations	Challenges dominant American value orientations
Criterion for Problem Selection	Theoretical importance		Social importance of segmental problems	Social importance of fundamental issues
Theoretical Perspective	Functionalism		Pragmatic liberalism	Humanism
Methodology	Logic and mathematics	Rigorous statistical analysis	Statistical and qualitative analysis	Disciplined insight
Criteria of Adequacy	Coherence	Correspondence	Usefulness	Perceptiveness
Intellectual Product	Analytical schemes	Empirical generalizations	Implications for action	General trends and tendencies

SOURCE: Marvin Bressler, "The Conventional Wisdom of Education and Sociology," in Charles H. Page, ed., *Sociology and Contemporary Education*, Random House, New York, 1964, p. 99. Reprinted by permission.

cation. Recently, however, trends similar to those in sociology have brought statistical empiricism into educational study. Educationists are beginning to raise significant questions about the process and content of formal education.

Uprisings on campuses of colleges and high schools throughout the world demonstrate that students have also begun to raise significant questions and to take action in regard to educational matters. Student revolts of current times have been ascribed to a variety of causes,[19] but have one common effect: they have stimulated sociologists of education to rethink scientific and humanistic analyses of the nature and process of education.

Sociologists utilize specific research methods which are common to other social sciences and to history. There are several classifications of these methods of inquiry.

1. *Content analysis*: similar to historical or literary studies in that documents are analyzed
2. *Observation and participation*: involvement ranging from detached descriptions of single-incident phenomena to longitudinal studies conducted while participating actively in the observed situations over an extended period of time
3. *Case studies*: collection and interpretation of descriptive information about a particular social group or institution
4. *Experimental research, laboratory form*: extensive control over the experimental environment, usually providing a means for comparison among sample groups
5. *Statistical analysis*: the utilization of mathematically derived formulas to test data for descriptions or inferences of relationships
6. *Logical inquiry*: inductive and deductive reasoning, arguments moving logically from general premises to specific conclusions or from specifics to generalizations
7. *Model building*: proposing theoretical models of social systems against which reality can be tested

It is difficult to determine the exact dimensions of the field of sociology. Some would include historical and psychological sociology, some would not. Some would limit the parameters to structural sociology, (which is sometimes difficult to define in itself), or sociological theory, or empirical sociology. The difficulty of definition which faces sociology is compounded in attempting to define the sociology of education.

NOTES

1. Jackson Toby, *Contemporary Sociology*, Wiley, New York, 1964, pp. 3, 4.
2. Ely Chinoy, *Sociological Perspective: Basic Concepts and Their Application*, Random House, New York, 1954, p. 1.
3. *Ibid.*, pp. 2–8.
4. *Ibid.*, p. 9.
5. *Ibid.*, pp. 2–8.
6. W. J. H. Sprott, *Social Psychology*, Social Science Paperbacks, Associated Book Publishers Ltd., London, 1962, p. xiii.
7. *Ibid.*
8. Caroline Rose, *The Study of Sociology*, Charles E. Merrill Books, Inc., Columbus, 1966, p. 6.
9. *Ibid.*, pp. 6–9.
10. Alex Inkeles, *What Is Sociology*?, Prentice-Hall, Englewood Cliffs, N.J., 1964, p. 12.
11. Auguste Comte, *System of Positive Polity*, vol. III, Carician-Coeury and Vor Dalmont, Paris, 1853; Longmans, London, 1876.
12. Joseph Roucek, ed., *Contemporary Sociology*, Peter Own Ltd., London, 1964, p. 5.
13. Inkeles, p. 33.
14. Roucek, p. 6.
15. C. Wright Mills, ed., *Images of Man: The Classical Tradition*, George Braziller, New York, 1960, p. 1.
16. Seymour M. Lipset, "Introduction," from T. H. Marshall, *Class, Citizenship and Social Development*, Doubleday, Garden City, N.Y., 1964, p. v.
17. *Ibid.*, pp. v, vi.
18. Marvin Bressler, "The Conventional Wisdom of Education and Sociology," in Charles H. Page, ed., *Sociology and Contemporary Education*, Random House, New York, 1964, pp. 100–105.
19. See Lewis Feuer, *The Conflict of Generations*, Basic Books, New York, 1969; Joseph Schwab, *College Curriculum and Student Protest*, University of Chicago Press, Chicago, 1969; James Kunen, *The Strawberry Statement*, Random House, New York, 1969; Charles Frankel, *Education and the Barricades*, Norton, New York, 1968; Jerry Avorn, *Up Against the Ivy Wall*, Atheneum, New York, 1969; and Harold Taylor, *Students Without Teachers*, McGraw-Hill, New York, 1969.

Chapter 2 / *The Relation of Sociology to Education*

The value of using sociological means to understand education, and of using education as a social construct for testing sociological theory and practice was discussed in Chapter 1. The rapid expansion of cross-field studies, titled either *educational sociology* or *sociology of education*, attests to the common interests of sociologists and educationists in describing, classifying, and analyzing the processes of education. Like the early workers in sociology, the first educational sociologists stressed the moralistic value of education or the very practical application of sociology to educational problems. More recently, sociologists of education have adapted the scientific methods of study used in sociology to their studies of the school.

The Debate over Approach

Brookover and Gottlieb argue that educational sociology is essentially a technology, while sociology of education is more scientific. They state that the main concerns of educational sociology have been viewing education as

1. a means of social progress
2. a basis for deciding the objectives of education
3. an applied sociology
4. an analysis of the socialization process
5. a training for educational workers
6. an analysis of the place of education in society
7. an analysis of social interactions within the school and between the school and the community.[1]

Brookover and Gottlieb contend that in each of these interests the educational sociologist has been concerned only with the aspects of sociology applied to problems in schools. The result has been the development of a technology which was intended to impart specific instructions to educators as to how they should operate education. Brookover and Gottlieb maintain that the newly developing sociology of education is the product of the thinking of sociologists from the late 1920s on, who stressed the "pure science" aspects of sociology and denied the applied, "human" portions. This scientific approach is more in line with the movement in sociology toward the refined instruments and value-free analysis treated earlier.

Ronald Corwin suggests that "sociologists study education for the same reasons that they study business, medicine, the family, and other institutions: to determine how much of the institution can be explained from a sociological perspective and to satisfy their curiosity about that institution in the process."[2] The difference between education and these other fields, however, is that education already had its own researchers and modes of study, so that educational sociology emerged as a union of both sociology and education which was difficult to define. Corwin notes the moralistic development in early educational sociology and the use of the term *sociology of education* to signify the later development of scientific theory.[3]

Early work in sociology of education stemmed from the interests of the founders of sociology: Comte, Spencer, Dewey, Ross, Cooley, and especially Durkheim.[4] E. George Payne, who founded the *Journal of Educational Sociology* in 1928, noted disagreement over both the value of sociological study for education and the type (if any) of sociology that would be valuable.[5] To emphasize the importance of studying educational sociology for students preparing to teach, Payne quoted a statement made in 1893 by William T. Harris that "No philosophy of education is sound unless based upon sociology." In 1934, he described the movement of educational sociology toward scientific methods:

. . . the trend of educational sociology . . . toward refinement in method in accordance with scientific techniques, and toward a definition of problems in terms of the measurement of the results of educational processes for social efficiency. . . . The trend has been in the direction of regarding educational sociology as belonging to the field of sociology rather than to education, and to use the better techniques of the sociologists in educational research.[6]

Sociology has advanced sufficiently as a science to warrant us saying that no adequate educational program can be constructed, no educational procedure can be justified, and no educational techniques can be effective if the scientific data provided by sociology are omitted from consideration.[7]

These are statements supportive of the move to scientific sociology of education, but they still bear traces of the tradition of a moralistic approach to educational situations.

Dan Dodson, reviewing changes in educational sociology during the quarter century preceding 1952, noted the following:

1. Change in emphasis from teaching and learning to growth and development
2. Development of knowledge of the meaning and function of culture
3. Increased understanding of the impact of social change
4. Increased understanding of groups and group processes related to education
5. Increased understanding of the dynamics of social class in relation to schools and children
6. Explosion of the myth of racial superiority
7. Increased knowledge of the impact of the community on the school[8]

Orville Brim concluded that the contributions of sociological research on education include both solutions to practical problems of education and continued growth of general social theory. In describing the relation of sociology to education, Brim stated:

> For the sociologist, the formal educational system of this country constitutes what is probably the richest and most accessible natural source of raw data on personality and social interaction; it needs only to be systematically mined by careful research. For the educator, the important issues he faces in his daily work center almost without exception on interpersonal relations—between teachers, between pupils, between teacher and pupil, between faculty and community—and the continuing attention of the sociologist to such issues cannot fail to illuminate and sharpen one's understanding of these specific social processes.[9]

More recently, Donald Hansen has suggested that the current movement toward cooperative ventures between the two fields is both desirable and dangerous.[10] The desirability stems from similar interest in the analysis of educational phenomena. The danger emerges, according to Hansen, from the traditional divergence of operating premises, methodologies, and expected results of the two fields. He contends that the basic dividing point is in the different modes of inquiry: education has developed as a *normative* inquiry while sociology tends to be *empirical.* The distinction that Hansen draws here is similar to the earlier discussion of the move from moralistic to scientific analysis in both sociology and education. That is, the normative mode of inquiry is based on the assumption that prescribed desirable goals of organization, behavior, and purpose are available and can be established as norms against which the school can be evaluated. Empirical inquiry, as Hansen explains it, "is dedicated to the establishment of verified knowledge, internally consistent, cogent, and adequate to its subject."[11] Hansen argues that both normative and empirical theory are important to the study of education and suggests, in a position similar to that of Brookover and Gottlieb, that educational sociology be used to describe the normative approach to educational theory and practice, while sociology of education be used to describe the empirical method.

The essential difference, then, seems to be one of varying perspectives of the investigator, whether in the field of sociology or education. If, as this treatment suggests, the field of education is also undergoing a movement toward empirical data gathering and analysis, then the specific title given to the study may not be particularly important, so long as it is realized that both sociology and education are multiple-approach fields. Arguments over which approach is most valuable rage in both sociology and education. C. Wright Mills[12] and Peter Berger[13] contend that there is a need for a humanistic or social-action–oriented sociology which accepts and develops normative theory. Such prominent sociologists and educators as David Riesman, Edgar Z. Friedenberg, Paul Goodman, and William Whyte demonstrate that it is possible to utilize empirical data to define, establish, or alter social norms.[14]

The Need for Objective and Subjective Viewpoints

This book is predicated on the belief that the study of education as a social enterprise—functionally, structurally, culturally, socioeconomically, and politically—is enhanced and illuminated by the active involvement of value and nonvalue sociologists and educators. The subjective-objective dilemma of education and sociology is not theirs exclusively. Maurice Natanson, in a pedagogically oriented book of readings on this problem of approach to social phenomena, indicates that the problem pervades all the social sciences, but presumably does not prohibit the contributions to social understanding from all approaches.[15] He notes that the "dialectic between 'objective' and 'subjective' approaches to social reality is a gross oversimplification of the actual situation."[16] This view supports the general position taken here in relating sociology to education. On the positive side, the intellectual battle in the social sciences between empiricists and normative or subjective philosophers has merely increased the opportunities for examination and evaluation of educational problems.

If the school, for example, has a social obligation to transmit the accumulated wisdom of a culture to youth, then subjectivists can analyze and utilize the means available to accomplish this task. Empiricists may consider the extent to which measurable parts of that wisdom are imparted and the relative efficiency of the various means of transmission without regard to good or evil. On a more practical level, if a subjectivist surveys the social milieu and prescribes that teachers should be drawn from lower social-class backgrounds because of assumed affinity to students of lower social classes, empiricists should undertake the collection and analysis of data in an attempt to verify or deny that position. The need for theory, research, application, and evaluation in education is so great, and the present state of knowledge about educational problems is so limited, that sociology of education and educational sociology both have substantial contributions to make.

It is important, however, that the student of sociology as related to education understand the complexities of the objective-subjective continuum, because the comprehension and utilization of generalizations derived from sociological or educational investigations depend upon the perspective of the investigator and the reader. Thus, it is very easy for an unsophisticated teacher or student to accept findings and conclusions from moralistic or empirical studies without thoroughly reading the logic or data, or appreciating the differing perspectives. This often happens when the student becomes a teacher or a school critic and puts into practice a limited viewpoint based upon superficial understanding; the result may be the notion of a single, simple, right answer to a complex social problem. No book can eliminate this problem; the goal here is simply to create an awareness of and a sensitivity to education as a social institution, process, and activity which is subject to sociological analysis.

Problems Confronting the Sociology of Education

The problems confronting the sociology of education are similar to those of any field which attempts to make practical application of the theoretical framework of a parent discipline. The first problem is to determine the direction and focus of interest of the field. Sociology and sociologists can remain largely independent of outside pressures if they wish, although interest in the acquisition of grants from the government, industry, and private funds limits this independence. Sociologists of education, however, must be dependent upon the needs of the schools in determining their direction. Schools of education have long felt that their primary function is to serve the schools. The result of this lack of independence and emphasis upon service to schools has been to limit the research and thinking of many sociologists of education to the practical, immediately applicable aspects of the field. Primary research and theory, which may have no immediate value to the schools, has been neglected. On the other hand, much of the research which has been done by sociologists of education has not been practical enough to suit some school personnel. Thus sociology of education often has been neither here nor there—neither independent enough to engage in primary research nor practical enough to give immediate, concrete advice to schools.

The second problem facing sociology of education is to determine the use or purpose of the field. Sociology of education has neither the prestige of the parent discipline nor the immediate practical application of curriculum or school administration. The field, therefore, must often defend itself in the academic community, even while striving to maintain contact with the affairs of the schools. Sociology can clothe itself in the mantle of respectability by indicating its age, its purely theoretical aspects, and its vast work in the empirical realms. Sociology of education, however, is not an old field; it must have practical value if it is to remain in the realm of education; and empirical study has been sadly lacking. Also, whereas curriculum, administration, counseling, and guidance have been able to indicate their practical value to the educational community, sociology of education has not. Students who are required to study curriculum design or educational psychology can see the relevance of these two fields; the former tells them what to do with the children, and the latter tells them about the development and learning experiences of the children. Sociology of education is not that immediately practical. Rather it is practical on a secondary level. For example, the study of the structure of institutions is of little practical value in and of itself to the student of education who has been assigned to a class in educational sociology. When sociological dynamics peculiar to the school are made clear to him, however, it is possible that he will deal with parents, administrators, and himself in a different way. Through studying how the community, the specific parent, the administrator, the teacher, and the student must interact because of the structure of the institution of which they are all members, the teacher may require different perspective in dealing with all the principal parties involved. The basic problem is that little if any of the material covered in a course in educational sociology can be of relevance unless the student wishes to make it part of his relevant "apperceptive mass." Teachers of educational sociology could discuss the social structure of the school, and many students would still see no relation between their own teaching and what was discussed in class. Because our society as a whole has not learned to think in sociological dimensions, it is difficult for the student to make the language of sociology relevant to his work and life.

Because sociology of education is not fully developed, independent, or practical, it perhaps has more in common with such fields as industrial sociology and some of the public administration "spinoff" areas than it does with either sociology or education. Sociology of education must still prove to its academic critics that it has content, and it must prove to its educational critics that there is practical value within that content.

With these two problems in mind, what are the parameters of sociology of education? First, of course, is the area of research—the attempt to apply some of the methods of sociology to the field of educational research. In the recent past, the most damaging criticism leveled at education is that most of what passes for research is unreliable because of the methods of sampling, the statistical procedures used and misused, and the inability to control variables. The sociological techniques of analysis and investigation can improve the quality of educational research. This is not to imply that education should or could become a purely empirical science, but rather to bring educational research out of the "show and tell" stage.

The second general area of sociology of education can be seen in the problems of the subareas of sociology such as criminology, race relations, and deviant behavior, and the way in which they relate to the role of the school.

The third general area is perhaps the most specific. Here the emphasis is upon the school itself as it functions within the larger society. This includes the study of the school as a social system, the cultures of the school, and the institutional practices of the school.

Summary

In brief, the purposes of sociology of education, or educational sociology, are: (1) to assume with modifications a methodology and methodological principles from sociology and use them to enhance educational research; (2) to investigate the relation of specific sociological areas such as deviant behavior, race relations, and criminology to the role of the school; and (3) to study the school as it interrelates with the rest of society.

NOTES

1. Wilbur Brookover and David Gottlieb, *A Sociology of Education*, American Book, New York, 1964, pp. 5–10.
2. Ronald G. Corwin, *A Sociology of Education*, Appleton-Century-Crofts, New York, 1965, p. 55.
3. *Ibid.*, pp. 56–66.
4. *Ibid.*; Emile Durkheim, "The Dualism of Human Nature and Its Social Conditions," in Kurt H. Wolff, ed., *Emile Durkheim, 1858–1917*, Ohio State University Press, Columbus, 1960; Emile Durkheim, *Education and Sociology*, Free Press, New York, 1956; and A. J. C. Ottoway, "Emile Durkheim and Educational Sociology," *British Journal of Sociology*, 1957, pp. 153–165.
5. E. George Payne, "Sociology and Education," *The Journal of Educational Sociology*, vol. 12, no. 6, February, 1939, pp. 321–327.
6. E. George Payne, *Readings in Educational Sociology*, vol. 2, Prentice-Hall, Englewood Cliffs, N.J., 1934, p. 732.
7. Payne, "Sociology and Education," pp. 323–324.
8. Dan W. Dodson, "Educational Sociology Through Twenty-Five Years," *The Journal of Educational Sociology*, vol. 26, no. 1, September, 1952, pp. 2–6.
9. Orville G. Brim, *Sociology and the Field of Education*, Russell Sage Foundation, New York, 1958, p. 7.
10. Donald A. Hansen, "The Uncomfortable Relation of Sociology and Education," in Donald Hansen and Joel Gerstl, eds., *On Education—Sociological Perspectives*, Wiley, New York, 1967, pp. 3–36.
11. *Ibid.*, p. 16.
12. C. Wright Mills, *The Sociological Imagination*, Oxford University Press, Fair Lawn, N.J., 1959.
13. Peter L. Berger, *Invitation to Sociology*, Doubleday, Garden City, N.Y., 1963.
14. See such works as: David Riesman, *The Lonely Crowd*, Yale University Press, New Haven, 1950; *Abundance for What?*, Doubleday, Garden City, N.Y., 1964; *Individualism Reconsidered and Other Essays*, Free Press, New York, 1954; *Constraint and Variety in American Education*, University of Nebraska Press, Lincoln, Nebr. 1956. Edgar Z. Friedenberg, *Coming of Age in America*, Random House, New York, 1965; *The Dignity of Youth and Other Atavisms*, Beacon Press, Boston, 1965; *The Vanishing Adolescent*, Beacon Press, Boston, 1959. Paul Goodman, *Compulsory Miseducation*, Horizon Press, New York, 1964; *Growing Up Absurd*, Random House, New York, 1960; *People or Personnel*, Random House, New York, 1965. William H. Whyte, *The Organization Man*, Simon and Schuster, New York, 1956.
15. Maurice Natanson, ed., *Philosophy of the Social Sciences: A Reader*, Random House, New York, 1963.
16. *Ibid.*, p. ix.

PART II

MODELS FOR ANALYSIS OF THE SCHOOL

This part is specifically designed to give the student four models which it is hoped will help him to judge his situation and to be more effective in it. It should help the teacher to understand and analyze the behavior of his students and his superiors; in this way he should be able to aid the learning process of one and stay in the good graces of the other.

Though many of the examples given in the four models relate to education and the schools, the models themselves are not taken from educational theory and are very broad in their approach. Little attempt has been made to give answers to the specific problems which will confront the teacher. Rather, the purpose of this section is to present broad analytical models which are applicable to many situations. All four models are not equally efficacious in all situations; in any given situation, however, at least one of the four should apply.

There are five chapters in Part II. Chapter 3 deals with the general characteristics of institutions and gives a background for the chapters to follow; Chapter 4 discusses the school as an administrative unit, using the work of Guba and Getzels as the theoretical base; Charter 5 develops the Marxian constructs of history, class, and spheres of influence as a model for analyzing the school; Chapter 6 analyzes the school as a total institution, as described in the works of Goffman; and Chapter 7 discusses the school as a culture, using the works of Hall and Trager as a theoretical base.

It should be noted that the theoretical nature of this part does not lend itself to the detailed footnotes of Part I. Therefore, in place of footnotes, a bibliography citing the most basic works has been supplied at the end of each chapter.

Chapter 3 / *What Is an Institution?*

Defining the Institution

We often think of institutions in terms of physical organizations, that is, as a school, a mental hospital, a veteran's home, and so forth. There are many institutions, however, which are neither physical nor organizations in the usual sense. Marriage, democracy, or particular behavioral patterns within organizations which have become traditional are also institutions. An institution is *any belief, construct, organization, or being which, through historical circumstance, has become identified with a certain set of functions and behaviors.* For example, the family is an institution in that, in our culture, the family is connected with a set of functions and behaviors. For example, it is monogamous; there are usually progeny; there is an extension of the immediate family in that there are also grandparents, uncles, and so forth; and there is a certain amount of privacy connected with the family in that certain behaviors are expected to be carried out in private. Both nonphysical and physical institutions have functions and behaviors.

Characteristics of the Institution

Though there are many characteristics which can be used to describe institutions, there are seven which seem to be generally accepted as being inherent in all institutions.

FUNCTIONS

The first characteristic is that all institutions have functions; that is, they do something and what they do has some relationship to what they are supposed to do: schools are supposed to teach and legislative bodies are supposed to legislate. Functions, according to Merton, generally are either *manifest* or *latent*. The manifest function of an institution is the overt, generally understood function for which the institution is originally established and the function which the institution is supposed to perform. The latent function is generally less understood and is not nearly so overt. It is, however, more basic in that it is often more effectively performed than the manifest function. An example will serve to illustrate the difference. During the 1850s in Great Britain there was a depression of rather grave proportions. One of the most serious problems was that there were many men out of work. Since women could often be hired at a lower rate then could men, they were often preferred by employers. This heightened the depression, particularly in industrial areas and major cities. Prostitution, however, turned out to be more profitable than working in factories, so many women (an estimated 50,000) took to walking the streets. The manifest function of prostitution is more or less obvious and does not need to be discussed here. The latent function of prostitution at this particular time was to take some women out of the legitimate labor market and force industry to employ the higher paid men, since women were not available. In this way the latent function of prostitution was to ease the severity of the economic depression. Suffice it to say that the first characteristic of institutions is that they have functions.

ACTORS

The second characteristic of institutions is that they have actors (people or other participants) to carry out their functions. Though the actors who perform within the institution are indispensable (the institution could not function without them), it should be pointed out that the interest of sociology and social structure is less with the actor himself than with how he fits into the system. For example, that a particular actor may or may not be neurotic is of little or no concern in the study of social structure. What is of concern is how that neurosis affects his behavior, the behavior of others, and the institution. An administrator who feels that everything must be in its correct place and that every person must conform to a set of rules and regulations is not interesting clinically because of his neurosis but rather because he causes certain characteristics to develop within the institution which he leads. As another example, a computer center is an institution with both latent and manifest functions in which one of the primary actors is the computer itself. The computer can either function with great simplicity and efficiency or be cumbersome, irritating, and exasperating. Computers can be either "intelligent" or "stupid." Again, however, the sociologist's interest is not in the intelligence of the computer but rather in how the computer's behavior affects the behavior of other actors and what is its overall effect on the computer center.

A SHARE IN THE SOCIETY

The third characteristic of institutions is that they share in the society of which they are a part; that is, institutions exist not in a vacuum but as part of the greater society. Each institution is interrelated with many others just as, for example, the grammar school is related to the high school, the junior high school, the political structure which finances it, and the community which supports or censures its programs. All these institutions (the school, the body politic, the community, etc.) share certain core values and ideas about what should go on in a school, what the society in general should be like, and how the school can increase or decrease that societal dream. For example, though punctuality and attendance are not usually considered part of the curriculum of the schools, society expects that they be taught to the young. For this reason, the schools are expected to train the students to come to school and to be on time. They are also expected to keep records so that the business and military establishments will be able to judge how well the student has learned these two important roles. There may be a number of teachers and principals who find that taking roll is a detriment to learning since it imposes upon the time and the atmosphere of the classroom. However, the schools are part of the broader culture and therefore must maintain and transmit the commonly held values of that culture. An example of a more academic nature might be the difference in history books in different parts of the country, or in different countries, since it is the prerogative of local and national school boards to support commonly held norms regardless of historical fact.

STRUCTURE

The fourth characteristic of institutions is that they have structure; that is, they have organizations which can be determined and analyzed. The organizational pattern with which we are most familiar is the overt one. The manifest organizational chart is usually quite simple and straightforward since there is a chain of command which can be easily followed by an observer. In military organizations, for example, the chain of command manifestly runs from the Commander-in-Chief (President of the United States), through the Joint Chiefs of Staff, various generals, colonels, majors, captains, lieutenants, and down to the lowly buck private. The latent chain of command, however, is far more devious and far more effective. For example, a corporal who types out orders can, and often does, have a great deal of power in determining which memoranda he feels are important enough for his commander to see and which are not. This is part of the covert chain of command which often is the real determining force in decision making. In education, the principal who listens to the janitor because he has been around longer than anyone else and his brother-in-law is on the school board is exemplifying the use of a covert chain of command.

A further point concerning the structure of institutions relates to atmosphere, the viewpoint, or *Weltanschauung* of an institution. Each institution seems to have a peculiar tenor or feeling about it. One school will be more democratically run than another, even though they are in the same district, the principals are brothers, and the student bodies are largely of the same cultural backgrounds. There are nuances which distinguish institutions just as much as do organizational charts, objectives, or chains of command.

Another structural tendency in institutions is for persons who enter the institutions to step into pre-existent roles. The actor who has been asked to join the institution will be expected to "fill a particular slot" and to fulfill certain expectations of those who are already there. He will to some small extent be able to change his role by introducing his personality into it, but his deviation will be limited by institutional pressures. A wife, for instance, expects her husband to behave in certain characteristic ways. Many of these behaviors have little or nothing to do with her individual spouse, but rather have to do with the pre-existent role which society holds to be part of the role "husband." The wife shares the belief in these roles and in turn expects her husband to believe in them. If he behaves in a contrary fashion, he will be considered a "bad husband."

SANCTIONS

This last example touches upon the fifth general characteristic of institutions: namely they are sanction-bearing. Any institution can give either rewards or punishment for the behavior of its actors. If the actor does not defy the structure and assumes the role which has been set for him by the institution, he will receive praise or at least no blame. If the actor defies the structure and does not wish to assume the role presented, however, the institution will attempt to force him into the structure and role through punishments of some sort. If the deviant behavior continues, the institution can censure and eliminate the actor from its ranks.

RESISTANCE TO CHANGE

It is possible, of course, for the actor to attempt to change the role. This generally proves to be difficult, since institutions tend toward conservatism. If the institution changes, it must in some ways have been ready to change, in which case the actor is not really changing the role; he may even have been brought into the institution expressly in order to change the role. This is often the case when a new executive is brought into a corporation which has shown less than potential strength, and when the present members of the institution feel that they are too identified with the *status quo* to foment massive change. For this reason, another actor may be brought in to initiate change. This function may be latent, in that even those who are directly involved may not have so diagnosed their motives and may not be fully aware of their desire for change.

Another method of changing a role is to convince the present members of the institution that a change is in order. In this case, the actor who wants a change must gauge how much change the institution will be willing to accept and in what direction that change will be most welcome. It is also imperative that the actor understand both the overt and covert structure of the institution so that he will know which actors will be needed for support and which can be ignored. By and large, this form of changing institutions from the inside after the arrival of a new actor is difficult in the extreme. Unless the actor is highly skilled, he will often find that in the long run he has only been able to accomplish as much change as the institution had originally sought.

3 Change in institutions experiencing rapid growth can occur when new actors outnumber the old actors and gain the power to implement change, not so much through the existing institution but rather by changing the structure, makeup, and *Weltanschauung* of the institution. Nevertheless, this too is an unusual situation.

4 Another method of change comes entirely from outside the institution. Here the society in general, or at least that portion of society which is in significant contact with the institution, changes emphasis and thereby insists upon change within the institution. For example, during the past few years there has been a great emphasis on science education. This change was not brought about through internal decision within the educational system but rather through a change in national policy and world politics.

STATUS

The last general characteristic of institutions is that they impart status; that is, certain assumptions are generally made about actors because of their membership in a particular institution. For example, there is no reason to assume that a graduate of a university is necessarily a better student, a better potential employee, or a better person than a junior college transfer to a state college or a graduate of a small liberal arts college. If, however, the society in general and the individuals involved tend to think of the university as being more prestigious and desirable, its graduates are also more prestigious and desirable. It is the institution which imparts this status and not the abilities of the actor himself. As another example, there are some companies and institutions of higher education which will not hire, or prefer not to hire, unmarried men because they believe that unmarried men are less stable than married men. The fact that this is not necessarily so, and further, that stability may have little or nothing to do with success in the position is disregarded. The institution of marriage, or lack of it, gives a certain status to the actor, and others may act on the basis of that status rather than on the relevant characteristics and qualifications of the actor.

Summary

An institution, then, is any belief, construct, organization, or being, which, through historical circumstances, has become identified with a certain set of functions and behaviors. Institutions may be physical or ideational. Institutions have many characteristics, of which seven of the most basic are that: (1) they have functions (both latent and manifest), (2) they have actors who carry out these functions, (3) they share in the society of which they are a part, (4) they are structural, (5) they are sanction-bearing, (6) they resist change and (7) they impart status.

The four chapters which follow provide four methods of analyzing institutions. The first method concerns the institution as an administrative unit; the second deals with the institution as a sphere of influence; the third with the institution as a total institution; and the fourth deals with the institution as a culture.

BIBLIOGRAPHY

Donald Martindale, *The Nature and Types of Sociological Theory*, Houghton Mifflin, Boston, 1960.

Robert K. Merton, *Social Theory and Social Structure*, rev. ed., Free Press, New York, 1956.

Talcott Parsons, Edward Shils, Kaspar D. Naegele, and Jesse R. Pitts, eds., *Theories of Society*, 2 vols., Free Press, New York, 1961.

Chapter 4 / *Administrative Style and the Individual Actor*

This chapter deals with the administrative style of institutions. The object of this chapter, like that of Chapters 5 and 6, is to provide a method of analyzing how the institution attempts to maintain stability and control over its member actors. This chapter, however, deals specifically with the effects of administrative style on the individual actor. The model used is adapted from the Guba-Getzels construct.

The administrative model attempts to determine how and why institutions can vary the behavior of their members, and how these members react to such manipulation. As mentioned before, every institution is part of the greater social system. The members as well as the institution itself respond to the pressures, norms, and values of their greater society; indeed this is where all behavior, both individual and institutional, begins. Most behavior, however, is effected or even molded by the institution. This molding process is the subject of this chapter. The various forms it can take are shown in Table 3, which should be studied carefully since it will be referred to throughout the chapter.

Before beginning the discussion, let us define the three main

TABLE 3

Subjective Categories of Institutional Modes

Institutional Mode	Center of Attention in Each Mode	Character of Roles and Personality in Each Mode	Behavior Within Roles in Each Mode
NOMOTHETIC	Role and role expectations of *institution*	Role: Defined in terms of *role expectation*; dynamic organization outside the actor	Overadjusted Underintegrated
			Adjusted Effective
TRANSACTIONAL	Roles and needs of both institution and indiv-idual	Balance of role expec-tation and need disposition	
			Integrated Efficient
IDEOGRAPHIC	Personality and need dispositions of *indi-vidual*	Personality: Defined in terms of *need disposition*; dynamic organization within the actor	Overintegrated Underadjusted

institutional modes: *nomothetic, transactional,* and *ideographic. Nomothetic* institutions are those which establish rules and regulations for the actors with or without their consent. The primary characteristic of this kind of institution is that the rules are determined prior to the individual actor's appearance. The chain of command is relatively determined and rigid, and moves from top to bottom. Both the ends and the means also are established, exist apart from, and antedate the actor who is asked to achieve the ends.

Ideographic institutions allow the individual actor to determine his own role. That is, in the ideographic institution the actor feels that he is free to establish the parameters of his own behavior and role after he has entered the institution. If there is a chain of command, it tends to be loose and not followed with any great care. If ends are established, they are usually determined by group discussion or by the actor establishing them himself. The means are equally fluid.

Transactional institutions fall somewhere between the other two. While the actor in such an institution feels that some of the ends and means are given, he also feels that many are left open and fluid and that he may exercise his choice in these open areas.

It should be emphasized, however, that all institutions are subjectively defined *by the actors* themselves as being nomothetic, ideographic, or transactional. That is, no institution is objectively one or another, and different actors may define the same institution differently or the same actor may define the same institution differently at different times. For example, following World War II the Armed Forces developed a far more liberal approach toward discipline, military regulation, drilling, and the importance of obedience. While most draftees and many volunteers approved the change from largely nomothetic to a more transactional approach, some members of the institution felt that the service was "going to the dogs," that it was becoming far too ideographic. A similar situation exists with regard to inmates' attitudes toward prisons, an institution generally defined as highly nomothetic. Some inmates feel uncomfortable in any but the most restricted institution and therefore find the prison quite comfortable, that is, transactional. It is impossible to categorize any given institution as nomothetic, ideographic, or transactional, since the definition depends on the perspective and the attitudes of the actor who is doing the defining.

With this extremely important distinction in mind, we can discuss nomothetic, ideographic, and transactional institutions and the styles of leadership within them. In this discussion our primary interest is in the behaviors of individuals within institutions, the behaviors of institutions toward their member actors, and the responses of one to the other. Our goal is a greater understanding of why certain behaviors are common in the interaction of individuals and institutions.

While the outcome of the interaction between individual and institution is behavior, it should be remembered that, as mentioned before, all behavior within and outside of institutions begins in the social systems. No behavior is performed in a vacuum. Behavior is based on the norms and values of the society in which the individual or institution performing them resides, and grows out of the milieu in which it is performed. When the behavior is performed, however, it also adds to that social milieu and becomes part of the mass which is the groundwork and the base for the next behaviors. All behavior emanates from and must add to the social system of which it is a part.

The Institution Versus the Individual

Within the social system, institutions are formed which perform functions needed by that social system (see Chapter 3). Institutions, because they do have functions and are interested in effective behavior, tend to be nomothetic in character; that is, they tend to establish *goals* and ends for an actor before he begins his role. Within the institutional structure, however, there is a countervailing force which causes the institution to modify its nomothetic behavior. This force is the individual who has needs and a personality which may be opposed to the roles and expectations established by the institution. The individual tends to want to establish, or at least have a hand in establishing, the ends and goals of his own role. The institution and the individual may or may not be in conflict. Regardless of the amount of tension, however, the individual and the institution are the two basic elements of this form of analysis and their interaction creates the basic behaviors to be studied.

Role Versus Personality

The analysis of the roles of individuals and their institutions discussed here is called *role theory* and is based largely on the work of Tomatsu Shibutani. Institutions establish roles for actors. Simply stated, a *role* is the sum of the behaviors expected of an actor by the institution. In order to understand the concept of a role fully, a number of subsidiary terms need definition. A *conventional role* is a prescribed pattern of behaviors expected of an actor in a given situation by virtue of this position. For example, a garbage collector is expected to act like a garbage collector, not like a college professor; the audience (other actors in the immediate vicinity who can observe the actor's behavior) and observers feel cheated when the two interchange their roles. In brief, a conventional role is what you are supposed to do because you are in that role.

A *role obligation* is a more specific statement of the conventional role. That is, the obligation is what the actor feels he must do because of his role. In part he performs the role consistently because he feels that it is right to do so; that is, the society has socialized the actor to believe that it is important for him to be consistent in his role. Another factor influencing him is the social pressure of the audience which expects him to maintain role consistency. The reason that role consistency is important to the entire institution and, for that matter, the society, is that so long as consistency is maintained, the behavior of a particular role incumbent is predictable. If each role incumbent were to establish his own ends, means, and behavior, no one would be able to predict the behavior of anyone else. This would make both societal and institutional functions complex and perhaps even unworkable.

As opposed to an obligation, a *role claim* is what the actor may expect others to do for him because of his role status (see Chapter 3). For example, a father has a number of obligations such as providing for his family, maintaining a semblance of discipline among offspring, and so forth. On the other hand, because of his role, he may demand the respect which his role deserves, for example, pipe, slippers, and a drink when he arrives home after a long day at the office or assembly line. As with many other roles, the role claims of the father are determined by how well he has fulfilled his role obligations. That is, he can make greater claims if he has fulfilled his obligations. The parental role, however, presents the aspect of change in roles and role behavior. This role, like many others in our society, changes as behavior of the incumbents changes, and so becomes slightly different for each generation of incumbents. Thus as each generation of fathers changes the traditional patriarchal pattern, their offspring are thereby even further removed from the original pattern.

Role playing involves the ability of the actor to live up to the claims and obligations of the role. In any role, the actor does not really need to believe in the value or justification of the role; he merely needs to follow it. The institution is concerned only with the actor's playing the role with adequate skill so that his functions can be performed. In a mass society it is entirely possible to play one role at one time and a totally different role at another. For example, the shop foreman who is a traditional working man to his fellow workers may be a typical middle-class suburban resident when at home. The roles may be quite different and he may believe in both, either, or neither. His belief is unimportant, however, in that the main interest of his boss, fellow workers, wife, children, and neighbors is the effectiveness with which he performs his roles.

Goffman, in *Presentations of Self in Everyday Life*, makes the distinction between sincerity and cynicism in role playing. In the former case the incumbent believes in the role, while in the latter he does not. No value judgment should be placed upon this distinction since at times sincerity can be bad and cynicism can be good. The example Goffman gives is that of a doctor who must decide whether or not to inform a patient that he has a terminal illness. The sincere thing to do would be to tell the truth and maintain the honesty expected of the doctor's role. However, cynicism, in this case lying to the patient about his condition, might be kinder. The point of Goffman's discussion is that we all play roles, and sometimes we believe in them and sometimes we do not.

Role taking refers to the ability of one actor to see the situation through the eyes of another. For example, the ability of a labor leader to see the situation from the standpoint of the industrialist is necessary if he is to know how much he can ask for without pressing the industrialist to the point of breaking off mediation, which is to the benefit of neither. Cooperation is based upon this ability to see a situation from the standpoint of the other actor. This does not mean that consensus is achieved through role taking, but only that consensus cannot be achieved without role taking. For example, the purpose of a marriage counselor is not so much to bring two people together as to get both to see the situation which seems to be bothering them from the perspective of the other. If this can be done, then the two partners will be able to communicate significantly, not only about the specific problems which they think they have but also about the many other problems of which they may not be aware.

A final distinction which should be made regarding roles relates to the difference between personal and impersonal roles. In *personal roles* the claims and obligations of the role are changed to some extent by the actor occupying the role. In *impersonal roles* the claims and obligations remain the same regardless of the actor's personality. For example, the head linesman in a football game generally is considered to occupy an impersonal role; that is, his job is simply to move the first-down markers when necessary and to spot the ball. By and large all head linesmen perform their functions in the same way; this would indicate that the role is an impersonal one. However, each head linesman behaves in a slightly different way. One runs when he moves the first-down markers, another walks, and another saunters with an air of special knowledge—each makes the role more personal.

Perhaps a more applicable example is the difference in the way curriculum materials are handled on the high school and university levels. In general the high school teacher is expected to follow a preestablished curriculum. The curriculum can be very demanding and time consuming, leaving the teacher little time for innovation, or it can be more flexible. In either case, the curriculum usually is followed quite closely. On the university level quite often the only curriculum guide presented to the teacher is the title of the course; the teacher is expected to "*wing it.*" The high school teacher's role tends by definition to be more impersonal than does the college teacher's role.

As institutions are juxtaposed to individuals, so roles are juxtaposed to personality. *Personality*, simply defined, is that portion of a person's behavior which though it does change over a long period of time, is still more or less constant from one situation to another. For example, one person tends to smile and laugh more than another regardless of the situation. This person is said to have a "happy" disposition or personality. Of course, this definition of personality is neither complete nor exclusive. Personality theory fits more justifiably within the domain of psychology than here. For the purposes of this discussion, however, the above incomplete definition is sufficient. For the model of institutions under discussion, the primary characteristic of personality is its opposition to the role established by the institution. Personality's primary function is to imbue the role with the individual, that is, to allow the individual to put part of himself into the role, even while performing the function which the institution has established.

Some institutions give the actor more opportunity than others to insert his personality. This can best be illustrated in the following schematic form:

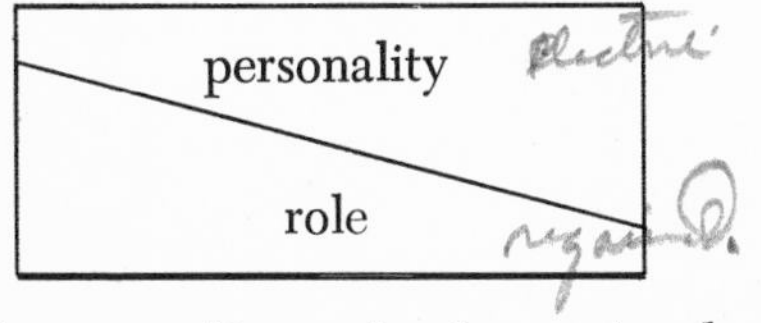

In all cases, both personality and role are involved; however, some institutions are traditionally role-oriented and others are traditionally personality-oriented. For example, mental hospitals are almost totally role-oriented, since the inmate is allowed little if any freedom to express himself. To a lesser extent the same can be said of the Armed Forces. Both of these would fall on the left-hand side of the schema. On the other hand, artist colonies and hippie retreats place far greater value on personality characteristics, on individual difference and freedom, than on function. These groups would fall on the right side of the schema.

Personality orientation is not necessarily better than role orientation, since, as with all nomothetic and ideographic categories, what is good, better, or best is determined through the perspective of the individual. Some people do not wish to emphasize their own personalities; they prefer an established role. Others find the established role limiting and prefer personality orientation.

The terms used in this discussion are *operationally defined*; that is, they are defined in terms of the behavior associated with them, not in any absolute sense. For example, personality is not defined in terms of some innate set of characteristics (through perhaps it could be) but rather in terms of the individual's behavior. A happy personality denotes happy role playing, not necessarily a happy inner self. (The inner self is the domain of psychology and is not germane to this discussion.) The same operationalism holds true for the description of roles. A role is not described as an absolute, but rather as a set of expected behaviors which can and often does change through personalization or change in societal attitudes.

From an operational viewpoint, then, a *role* is the dynamic organization of behavior outside the individual actor. It is dynamic in that it is constantly changing; it is organized since there is a set of expected behaviors which are joined to make up the role; and it is outside the actor since the role antedates the actor and will exist after he leaves it. A *personality* is the dynamic organization within the individual actor. The personality is also constantly changing and is also a conglomeration of patterns forming a whole. Unlike the role, however, it arrives at and leaves the institution with the actor.

If we wish to study the role and the personality of the actor more closely, we need to understand his role expectations and need dispositions respectively.

Role Expectation Versus Need Disposition

The closer one comes to "behavior" within roles in Table 3, the more complex the discussion becomes. This is because the table moves from the theoretical structure of the institution ("center of attention") to a more operational discussion of the interaction between the institution and the actor ("behavior with roles"). In discussing need disposition versus role expectation we must consider conflict within the institution and why and how it occurs.

Role expectations are the specific behaviors which are expected of an actor because he occupies a role. Whereas the role defines the actor's position in general terms (the teacher's role is to teach), the role expectation defines it in specific operational detail (the teacher's role expectation is to maintain order, teach history, and so forth). *Need dispositions* are those internal satisfactions which the actor expects to receive from his participation in the institution.

Both role expectations and need dispositions are defined in terms of adjusted and integrated behavior and in terms of efficient and effective behavior. *Adjusted behavior* is behavior which meets the role expectations, that is, behavior which is adjusted to the preexisting role expectation. *Integrated behavior* is behavior which meets the need disposition of the actor. In many cases a *rapprochement* between integration and adjustment can be achieved by compromise between the actor and the institution. In this case the individual is said to be effectively performing his function—doing what he is supposed to do—and doing so efficiently—using the least possible amount of emotional energy. *Effective behavior*, then, is doing what is expected, *efficient behavior* is doing it with a minimum of energy. Efficient behavior, refers to emotional, not physical, energy since the amount of physical energy expended seems to make little difference in terms of either the amount of work completed or the satisfaction to the actor.

Though the balance between adjustment and integration is often maintained, sometimes it is not. The first example of behavior in Table 3 shows one of the more common methods of dealing with a conflict between the need disposition of the individual and the role expectation of the institution: over-adjustment or conformity. In its extreme form, the individual subjugates himself completely to the institution. Often he will even forget the end for which the institution was designed and maintain a slavish dedication to his portion of the institutional process. An example would be the teacher who slavishly follows the course curriculum day by day, without thought as to whether her students are learning anything. The amount of overadjustment will, of course, vary with the individual and the institution; but to the extent that the actor overadjusts his behavior is underintegrated. His behavior is often very effective in that he does exactly what is expected of him, but his efficiency suffers in that his need dispositions are not satisfied and he is either emotionally "dead" or distraught.

The other extreme represented at the foot of the behavior column in Table 3, is known as overintegrated behavior. In this case the actor flaunts the institution and sacrifices effectiveness for his own internal efficiency. His behavior is under-adjusted and overintegrated. The institution often attempts to eliminate such an actor.

It must always be remembered that integrated and adjusted are subjective, relative terms; they are not absolute across institutions. What one institution will consider overintegrated behavior, another will consider just about right or even over-adjusted. Furthermore, what one actor considers overadjusted or overintegrated behavior may not be considered as such by another actor or his institution. Again we stress that this entire analysis is based upon the perspective or point of view of the individual or group actors or of the institution.

To repeat, there is no such thing as a nomothetic, an ideographic, or a transactional institution. There are only institutions which are considered nomothetic, ideographic, or transactional by particular individuals or institutions. If an actor feels comfortable and satisfied in an institution, then for him that institution is transactional. If that institution is satisfied with the way the actor performs his functions, then the behavior is considered effective and the actor is considered adjusted. The identical behavior in another actor, another institution, another time, or another place might be considered overintegrated or overadjusted, depending upon the perspective of the audience and the actor.

Transactional Behavior

The transactional category has not been discussed fully because it is the ideal. A transactional institution is one in which the actor and the institution have arrived at a balance which is mutually acceptable. This is not to imply that transaction is a middle path; it too can be quite extreme. For example, there is good reason to believe that every large institution needs certain people who slavishly follow the prescribed patterns: "There is a right way, a wrong way, and the Navy way; and we do it the Navy way." These are the clerks, the secretaries, the bureaucrats who keep the institution running because they will take the time and effort to do the little things which need to be done such as filing papers correctly, making out purchase requisitions, and keeping and balancing the books. Their behavior may be considered slavish and overadjusted by many observers, but the institution could not exist without these workers. Their role may indeed be transactional if it meets their needs as well as those of the institution, even though most of the audience may feel that the behavior is overadjusted and nomothetic.

An example of transactional behavior at the other end of the scale stems from an institution's need for new ideas if it is to grow. These ideas may come from the highly unconventional and overintegrated actor, but they are still important to the institution. Thus they are transactional in that they meet the needs of both the institution and the actor, even though each may irritate the other.

Summary

This chapter has attempted to provide another method of observing and analyzing institutions which may be applied to the school. The analysis is carried out in terms of the perspective or point of view of the institution and the actors within it. They can view behavior as nomothetic, ideographic, or transactional, depending on whether or not the individual or institution feels that the behavior is autocratic and restricting, individualistic and disruptive, or something between the two. Institutions, roles, and role expectations on one hand, and individual actors, personality, and need dispositions on the other are all factors in this analysis. Behavior can be described in terms of adjustment versus integration and overadjustment (underintegration) versus overintegration (underadjustment).

BIBLIOGRAPHY

Getzels, Jacob W., "Administration as a Social Process," in Andrew Halpin, ed., *Administrative Theory in Education*, University of Chicago, Chicago, 1958.

Getzels, Jacob W., and E. G. Guba, "Social Behavior and the Administrative Process," *School Review*, vol. 65, 1957, pp. 423–441.

Goffman, Erving, *Presentations of Self in Everyday Life*, Anchor Books, Doubleday, Garden City, New York, 1959.

Shibutani, Tomatsu, *Society and Personality*, Prentice-Hall, Englewood Cliffs, N.J., 1961.

Chapter 5 / *The School as a Sphere of Influence*

There are a number of conditions which differentiate this chapter from the other chapters in Part II. While the other chapters deal primarily with how the institution maintains stability, this chapter presents a model for the analysis of change. Also, while the authors of the theoretical formulations presented in the other chapters are modern, this chapter is based upon the works of Marx, particularly his *The Economic and Philosophic Manuscripts of 1844*, and *The German Ideology*. Since the original formulation is 125 years old, the language and the examples used by Marx are somewhat archaic and the immediate application somewhat more circuitous. The construct of spheres of influence is sufficiently important, however, that the difficulty of the immediate applicability is far overshadowed by the value of the model itself.

It is somewhat unfortunate that Karl Marx is known primarily as an economist rather than as a sociologist, for as the "father of Communism" he is either defended or attacked merely on the basis of his economic system. His model analyzing society and the institutions within the society is also a major contribution. Both defenders and attackers of Communism miss the point, that Marx and Engels were among the first sociologists who systematically looked at a society as the causal factor in the behavior of individuals, who argued that "man is made by history, not history by man."

In this chapter three constructs are presented: (1) the essential construct of all Marxian theory that the history of a society or institution determines the behavior of all its member actors, (2) the construct of the ruled versus the ruling classes, and (3) the construct of spheres of influence.

The Concept of History

In the Marxian construct of history, historical antecedents not only affect but are actually part of the present society. Each generation adds new constructs and new behaviors to the historical antecedents of previous generations and thereby adds not only to the history of the society but also to its present store of behaviors and existence. History then is a continuous process affected by many influences. Even a cursory inspection of today's college students' demands for an authoritative voice in determining policy on the college campus can be seen not only as an isolated movement of the 1960s but also as part of an historical-societal process. Within present student activism can be seen such antecedents as student involvement in civil rights and, prior to that, the mass higher education of lower-middle-class students through the GI Bill of Rights. Perhaps the college students' revolt can be projected in the future as having an effect upon the high school, where even today there have been isolated instances of high school students' strikes against the authority of the school.

One of the real difficulties in dealing with and analyzing the recent teachers' strikes in major metropolitan areas is that those in positions of power regard the teachers' strikes as relatively new and unusual phenomena. These strikes can be understood more easily if they are seen as part of a progression of growing professionalism among teachers. As salaries and prestige increase, the type of person who enters teaching tends to demand a greater respect from others. The behavior of teachers in negotiations with school boards is partially the outcome of a growing professional concern, for teachers are demanding not only more money but also smaller classrooms, better equipment, and even teaching assignments only in their own fields. In effect, they are demanding that the community, the school boards, and the superintendents give them an authoritative voice in the field which they know best: teaching and classroom behavior.

A further example of the relationship of spheres is that the teachers' strikes can be seen not only from the perspective of a growing professionalism among teachers but also from the perspective of a growing professionalism within the unions themselves. In the decades since World War II, unionism, as is the case with so many aspects of American life, has become increasingly middle class and semiprofessional in its behavior. This trend has made it possible for teachers to feel that they can maintain their professional status and still be militant unionists. The point here is not to attempt to determine the validity of unionism within teaching but rather to indicate that, if considered outside its historical context, the development of militancy and unionism among teachers is an unfathomable one.

The same kind of difficulty can beset a new teacher who sees a series of seemingly unconnected behaviors and attempts to deal with each one of these individually. It is only after he begins to see the individual acts as connected to those which preceded it and his own behavior as effecting any act that will occur in the future that he can understand the acts of others and his relationship to these acts.

Through this understanding that society and history are in many ways the same thing, an individual is capable of understanding the circumstances which determine his role and his behavior, his relationship to society, and therefore his ability to predict his own behavior as well as the behaviors of others. Any single behavior or movement of his is actually part of a much greater historical movement in that it has antecedents in the past and its present behavior will become an antecedent for future behaviors.

Thus Marx feels that: (1) society and history are the same; (2) man is made by circumstances, not circumstances by man; and (3) the sum of man's relationship to nature and to himself is handed down from one generation to the next, and with each new generation new inclusions are added to the mass.

The Concept of Class

The second major Marxian construct of interest to education is the differentiation between the ruled and the ruling classes. In Marxian theory the *ruling class* is defined in terms of wealth and its control of the means of production while the *ruled class* is determined by its lack of money and lack of control. In the present society the distinction based upon wealth has become somewhat vague with the rise of a relatively opulent middle class. Underlying Marx's construct of the ruling class, however, is the conception that this class controls and determines not only the means of production and the wealth of the society but also the norms of behavior of the society. The ruling class is the power elite not only in the area of wealth and commercial power but also in the law, the norms, and the behavior of the society. The ruled class then is distinguished by its inability to determine the norms of its own behavior; it has to follow the dictates of the ruling class. Within the school, for example, the ruling class may be made up of the community, Board of Education, principal, administrative personnel, and teachers, whereas the ruled class will include the powerless groups within the school: the students, incoming teachers, new principals, or new superintendents. Whatever group or person is not self-determining and must follow the dictates of a more powerful group is in the ruled class.

Whether or not a particular group is the ruling class will depend largely on the groups surrounding it and the specific time and situation in which it finds itself. As has already been implied, it is entirely possible for a person to be a member of a ruling group in one situation and a member of a ruled group in another. For example, the teacher who maintains control over his students in the classroom is the only ruling power within that classroom. As a corollary, his students are the ruled class. The positions are reversed, however, if the students can "take the class away from him." Through a systematic process of harassments and refusal to obey simple rules, the students can literally force a teacher to abdicate his position as ruler. Of course, nothing so extreme need occur for the teacher to change from a ruling to a ruled body. If the teacher is a probationary teacher and a principal enters the room, the students will often notice that the teacher changes his method of teaching, his method of dealing with students, and even his use of language and gestures. He has by the simple factor of one person's entering the room changed from a ruling to a ruled body.

This changeability of ruled and ruling classes makes it difficult for any actor entering a new institution to determine which groups or individual actors should be the models for his behavior. For example, the social leader in the teacher's lounge may indicate a set of behaviors which seem plausible in the smoking room; the incoming teacher assumes that since everyone recognizes him as the leader in that situation, his behavior should be emulated. When the new teacher attempts to follow the assumed dictates of the social leader, he often finds that the leader in the smoking room is not the leader in the teachers' meeting, in the department, or in any of the more academic aspects of the school. He may find that in order to understand what behaviors are acceptable, he must watch the football coach or a particular English teacher, or even the janitor if the janitor happens to be the recognized leader in that situation. The basic problem here is recognizing not only that there are ruled and ruling classes, but also that they change and an individual who is a ruling person in one situation may be a ruled person in another. An observer must be able to maintain such distinctions.

Institutions also may experience changes within the ruled and ruling classes. The power of a particular group or individual may be restricted either by the growing power of another group or the debilitation of its own group. This leads us to Marx's third major construct: the spheres of influence.

The Concept of Spheres of Influence

Marx's construct of change is quite different from that of other sociologists. Pareto, Weber, and others postulate the presence of forces outside the society to account for change within the society. As implied above, Marx believes that the seeds of most change (whether from a ruled class to a ruling class, or vice versa) are within the society itself. According to Marx, within each society there are germs of both equilibrium and change. Each generation is traditional in that it accepts most of the constructs of the previous generations and revolutionary in that it adds to this mass its own interpretations and, in some cases, new ideas and new constructs.

Each generation's influence on the following generations is measured by the extent of its sphere of influence. For example, in a highly tradition-oriented society, a son is expected to enter the occupation of his father. This pattern might be followed generation after generation, in which case the occupational sphere of influence is said to extend over many generations. In modern Western society a child's occupational choice is far less determined by the occupation of his father. In this case the sphere of influence of the father's occupation is extremely limited in time.

Conflict between differing spheres of influence occurs in any institution within a society. For example, one of the most serious conflicts facing many schools today is the difference in attitude between older teachers and those just entering the field. Much of the schools' activity, curriculum, and methods of discipline are within the sphere of influence of the older teachers and administrators. Many of the younger teachers, however, view teaching from a totally different perspective. One example of this generational conflict is the recent dispute over the curricular material of tenth-grade literature. The more traditionally oriented teachers feel that the students should be exposed to the great literature as traditionally defined, and would have the students read *Silas Marner* and *Julius Caesar.* Many of the new teachers, however, define great literature in a far less traditional sense and want their students to read *The Catcher in the Rye* and *Waiting for Godot.* This conflict is different from the conflict discussed in other chapters in that it is not so much a conflict of a specific area of culture or style of leadership as a far more general conflict involving underlying modes of operation and philosophies.

A society's or individual's sphere of influence, simply defined, is *the extent to which he can affect the lives and behaviors of others.* For example, universities pride themselves on their independence from governmental control. If one looks closely at the type of research in which universities are engaged, however, it can be seen that much of it is directly connected with government work. The reason, of course, is that the government, through grants, scholarships and research funds, can determine the kind of research financed and therefore the kind of research which will be done. Under these circumstances the university becomes the ruled class and the government becomes the ruling class. Universities are within the sphere of influence of the government to the extent that research is dictated by governmental funds. On the other hand, if a university should, through research, develop a new process or a new weapon, the history of that university then becomes part of the history of the national government and possibly the history of the world. Thus the academic discovery that it was theoretically possible to split the atom became part of the history of the United States through the Manhattan Project and shaped the history of the world at Hiroshima and Nagasaki. The sphere of influence had extended from a handful of scientists to the entire world.

The Power of Spheres

One of the drawbacks of the Marxian construct of spheres of influence is that Marx never distinguishes adequately between spheres which have great power and those which do not. Marx's only interest is in the distance that the sphere extends; to him a sphere which is greatly extended also has great power whereas a sphere which does not have great extension does not have great power. Although this analysis may be potentially valid, we know that in fact even two such great spheres as the United States and the Soviet Union have degrees of power within their spheres of influence.

In a short discussion in *Presentations of Self in Everyday Life*, Erving Goffman presents the hypothesis that the degree of *vested interest* in a particular sphere is what determines the extent of power which a society is willing to exercise. For example, the spheres of influence of the United States and of the Soviet Union both extend over most of the globe: the Soviet Union's influence extends even into the United States (for example, the tremendous interest in scientific education and in "getting to the moon first" after Sputnik) and the influence of the United States extends into the Soviet Union (the tremendous growth and interest in "Western" consumer products). Nevertheless, the degree of vested interest in a particular section of a sphere of influence varies greatly. When the Armed Forces of the Soviet Union entered Hungary after the Hungarian Revolt, there was a reasonable degree of certainty that the United States would not risk war by coming to the aid of the Hungarian people because our vested interest in the internal affairs of Hungary was not nearly so great as that of the Soviet Union. History repeated itself in Czechoslovakia, when the Czechs strove for more independence. Russia had a great deal to lose if either of these countries broke away from its sphere of influence. The United States, on the other hand, lost relatively little by not coming to their aid. When the United States discovered that Russian missiles were being brought into

Cuba, however, the vested interests of the United States were extremely great: Cuba is only 90 miles off the coast of Florida. Here the vested interest of the Soviet Union was not very great. When the United States demanded that the missiles be removed, placed an embargo upon Cuba, and boarded Russian ships, it had reason to believe that the Soviet Union would not forcefully intervene—Russia's vested interests were not nearly so great as those of the United States here.

This construct of strength of spheres of influence is directly applicable to the school. For example, most students are willing to recognize that even though they disagree with many of the superficial behaviors which are demanded of them in school such as punctuality, certain forms of dress, or speech patterns, they do not feel that their vested interests are sufficiently great in these areas to attack directly or attempt to thwart the school. That is, subconsciously the students realize that the school is more interested in having them obey these rules than they are in not obeying them. On the other hand, there are certain students who feel that the rules are so degrading that the strength of their vested interests becomes sufficiently great for them to attack the school directly. It is at this point that conflict arises, not so much because of the overlap of spheres of influence (indeed, they overlapped previous to the conflict) as because of the strength of the vested interest with which each party finds it necessary to imbue the sphere of influence. Under normal circumstances one or the other party is willing to retreat since the strengths of the vested interests differ. In certain situations, however, neither party is willing to back down, and then direct and frontal conflict over the spheres of influence occurs.

Summary

This chapter has combined the Marxian analysis of spheres of influence with the Goffman construct of the strength of vested interests within the spheres of influence. Marx's analysis is based on three interrelated constructs: (1) the concept of history and society as being one and the same process, (2) the distinction between the ruled and the ruling classes, and (3) the concept of spheres of influence.

Of particular concern to educators is an understanding of history, classes, and power of spheres with regard to their influence on school conflict. One of the difficulties which has most recently come to the fore is student-school conflict. In the past students were willing to assume the values of the school since the school's vested interest was far greater than that of the students. Recently, however, students and the community have gained a greater vested interest in their education and are therefore ready to challenge the authority of the school. Because of recent history (which has emphasized the importance of education among students and community) they are no longer willing to remain in the ruled class. The school, however, is largely unwilling to give a greater voice to students and the community, and sometimes seems to understand neither the conflict nor the genesis of it.

This chapter indicates methods of analyzing areas of potential conflict. It discusses the way in which change can occur *within* institutions, without interference from an outside, noninstitutional force.

BIBLIOGRAPHY

Fromm, Erich, *Marx's Concept of Man*, Ungar, New York, 1966.

Goffman, Erving, *Presentations of Self in Everyday Life*, Doubleday, Anchor Books, Garden City, N.Y., 1959.

Marx, Karl, Martin Milligan, trans., *The Economic and Philosophic Manuscripts of 1844*, International Publishers, New York, 1964.

Marx, Karl, *The German Ideology*, International Publishers, New York, 1939.

Chapter 6 / *The School as a Total Institution*

This chapter deals with power—specifically the power of the school over the student. It discusses the source of this power and its continuity, not only over the student's school life but also over his post-school life.

By power, we do not mean political power in the usual sense; the school is not known for its influence over society. Most changes in our society and in our schools have not come from within the schools but rather have been products of other institutions, such as space technology, universities, or the legislature. The type of power with which this chapter deals is not the power of the institution over the society, but rather the power of the institution to mold an individual. We do not place a value judgment on this molding process; we only seek to examine it so that we may understand the relationship of the school as an institution to its members.

Erving Goffman's analysis of the total institution in *Asylums* will be used as a model to demonstrate the school's power. As is the case with any model, it must be used with caution since one model for the investigation of institutions will not fit all cases.

Goffman discusses a particular type of institution: the mental hospital, which has almost total control over its inmates. The institution tells the inmate what and when he may eat, with whom he may speak, and even when he may fulfill his bodily functions. The total institution is, in short, an institution which governs the basic civilian functions of the individual member. The Army is the most familiar total institution, but Goffman finds the mental hospital a better example. Though our primary emphasis in this chapter is, of course, the power of the school over the individual, we shall retain Goffman's example of the mental hospital here because of its clarity. Once his theory has been stated, we can investigate its implications for the school.

The Deculturization and Reculturization Process

Since most actors are either not willing or not able to give up their individuality and previous cultural standards voluntarily, it is the task of the institution to "socialize" the potential inmate into acceptance. Though this process continues for as long as the inmate remains in the institution, the process is begun through *stripping or deculturization.* The object of the institution here is to eliminate the noninstitutional culture of the individual, which may contain practices which are at variance with the desires of the institution. This process begins even with admission procedures. Here the initial attempt is made by the institution to change the inmate from nonmember to member. First, physical objects which connect the inmate to his noninstitutional self are taken from him. In the mental hospital the inmate is informed that he may not retain his personal belongings, clothing, cosmetics, razors, and so forth. They are to be left with the authorities. The ostensible reason for this is to prevent the inmate from harming himself or committing suicide. According to Goffman, the actual reason is that individuality is connected with the "front" of personal belongings, and the institution must initiate the "de-individualizing" of the potential inmate. As another part of the stripping, the inmate is often told to undress in the company of others although he may never have done so before. He is then given a physical examination where he may be asked embarrassing questions about his personal and medical history. He then receives a uniform which is exactly the same as or at least similar to the uniforms of all the other inmates. In all these processes the individuality of the inmate is broken down so that he will be more receptive to the *reculturization* of the institution.

Reculturization is usually begun (1) by one member of the staff in a formal orientation in which rules of the institution and acceptable modes of behavior are explained, (2) through more personal contact with a particular member of the staff who has some close contact with the inmate during his stay, or (3) through observation of previously indoctrinated inmates. As part of the orientation, it generally is explained to the inmate that he will not be a successful member of the institution unless he conforms to the definition of acceptable behavior presented by the authorities. In the case of the mental hospital, it is implied not only that conformity is the only way to be acceptable to the authorities but also that the inmate will not get out of the hospital except by conforming to the authorities' definition of sanity. He therefore has a double reason for negating his own personality in favor of the personality definition presented by the institution.

Thus, through a process of stripping or deculturization before reculturization, the institution achieves conformity and a sense of membership among its inmates. In this way it achieves not a cure but rather an inmate which it can control with the least amount of effort. Some total institutions attempt to achieve this case of control for the society as a whole. For example, the Army cannot afford the luxury of individuals; it must have team members to function as a unit.

Usually the inmate takes one of four possible courses of action in order to counter the effects of the de-individualizing patterns of the institution:

1. *Situational withdrawal* in which the inmate apparently withdraws his attention from everything not directly concerning

himself and defines himself differently than does the institution

2. *Intransigent* line in which the inmate refuses to cooperate with the staff and is labeled a trouble maker. This is often the initial reaction of the inmate in response to inundation by the institution
3. *Colonization*, in which the inmate takes what little remains of his life outside the institution and defines his situation in terms of that part of his life. He redefines the norms of the total institution so that they will fit his picture of what life was like on the outside. He denies that there is any difference between his life outside and his present one, or he indicates that his present life is better than the one outside
4. *Conversion*, in which the inmate assumes the value structure of the institution as his own. He becomes the model patient, recruit, or student.

Regardless of which course of action the inmate takes, one of the themes which permeates his life in the total institution is that of the "underlife." The basic function of the "underlife" is to give the inmate the feeling that he is still maintaining some semblance of his individuality. This is accomplished by the development of series of procedures through which the less important rules—ones that are difficult for the institution to enforce—are broken. Thus the inmate may make obscene noises which cannot be traced to any one member of the group but which are distracting to the speaker and amusing to the other inmates. This type of behavior is relatively easy in the open wards of the average mental hospital. If an inmate is placed in a disciplinary ward, however, it becomes more difficult to engage in this behavior and consequently behavior becomes more bizarre.

Institutions can assume more or less total control. For example, a mental hospital controls more of the everyday activities of its inmates than does the Army, even though both are considered total institutions. The thing which distinguishes these two institutions is their degree of *permeability*. Permeability here refers to the degree of outside influence on the institution and its inmates. Even though there may be few outside influences which affect the soldier, he has periods of absence during which the Army has little control over his behavior as well as many periods during which he is allowed time to use as he sees fit.

The Power of the Schools

Schools, if we are willing to exclude restrictive boarding schools, are by no means so totally powerful as either the Army or a mental hospital. Yet there are enough similarities that the model of the total institution can be useful in analyzing the school's power over individuals. The school, though to a lesser degree, may display certain of the characteristics of the total institution:

1. An initial process of deculturization or stripping followed by the imposition of a set of norms and rules which might or might not have anything to do with outside norms. Thus school norms may have little or nothing in common with the family or peer norms of the student.
2. The four courses of action open to the inmate may be characteristic of the student population.
3. The student population may exhibit patterns of underlife. This would be particularly true of those students who are at odds with the patterns presented by the school authorities, but should to a lesser degree be true of all students.

Before beginning the discussion of the school as a total institution, it should be pointed out that although the term *total institution* might have a negative connotation, it should not be conceived in this light. For certain types of schools the "member" behavior of the students is of great importance. For instance, the highly academic setting requires that all the students follow the role prescribed by the teacher and adopt the silence necessary to hear the lecture. In such a school, the aspects of the total institution might so conform to the expectations of the students and the parents that there is little or no concern over what might be considered harsh treatment by more progressive educators. In any case it is important to remember that the purpose of this chapter is not to chastise the school for being a total institution, but rather to analyze the school in the light of the total institution so that it may be easier to understand the school's behaviors.

The previous background of the particular inmate is of little or no importance in studying the total institution, since the purpose of the institution is to mold the individual into a member who may differ markedly from the same individual as non-member. If the institution is wise, of course, it will take into account the inmate's background so that it will be able to control and analyze his behavior more effectively. The point to remember, however, is that the background is taken into account only in order to make the task of indoctrination easier. If, for instance, one of the goals of the school is to teach a particular behavioral pattern to the students (for example, punctuality or cleanliness), it will make little difference whether the child is a boy or girl, or from a lower- or upper-class family. The purpose is to teach the behavior, not to take into account the previous biography of the student. The school will take the child as he is and attempt to mold him into a "member." This is the purpose of a total institution.

Characteristic 1: The Culturization Process

This process is often begun before the child enters school. Regardless of the child's background, the child or his parents are told to fill out a series of registration forms. These forms involve information dealing with the child's parents, their occupation, if any ("If unemployed, for how long?"); the child's physical history (including any and all diseases), the parents' physical history, the number of siblings in the child's family, how many of these have attended the school, and so forth. All these items ostensibly serve the purpose of giving the school needed information regarding the child's academic ability. In many cases, however, it also gives the school a great deal of information which will help to pigeonhole or label the child. It also gives the parents and the children their first sign that the school is watching their behavior.

Once the student has passed the entrance requirements, he is placed with a group of children who may or may not be his peers. In some schools there is a definite, though often unwritten, policy that children of the same peer group (often called gangs) are to be separated as much as possible. This is done so that the teacher will have less trouble in handling the children. Within the class group, the child is informed, either formally or informally, of the rules and regulations of the institution. He is also informed that if these rules are broken, certain sanctions will be placed upon him or the group. These sanctions vary from writing a note to the parents to having him put his head on the desk while the other children play or even to sending him home.

Some of the rules and regulations will run counter to the behavior of the child in the nonschool setting. For example, toilet habits become a ritualistic pattern involving requests for permission (usually granted). Separation of the sexes into different rooms requires the child to memorize which room is correct and which is taboo (this creates a code of modesty); at the same time codes of modesty are broken down within the sex group by having the child go to the bathroom in the presence of others. All three of these patterns may be opposed to nonschool behavior. The child may also be told that he is to remain silent during the milk period, that he is to have a rest period, and so forth. Most of the rules and regulations presented to the primary school child are designed as a "breaking in" procedure. This procedure is not nearly so severe as is the deculturization of the mental hospital inmate, but it serves the same function: to mold each person into a member who can be handled easily by the institution.

If the school finds that it cannot form the child into a member, the parents are called in. They are informed of the school's opinion of the child's behavior and are given pessimistic predictions for his future should this behavior continue. The kindergarten teacher informs the parents not only of the consequences of the behavior for the first grade performance, but also of its consequences if it is carried over into adult behavior.

The behavior and the parents' attitude are duly noted in the child's cumulative folder which will follow him through his academic career, even if he moves from that school. This leads to the "looping" process described by Thomas Scheff whereby behavior in one situation will be brought to the child's attention in another (looping and labeling concepts will be more fully discussed in Chapter 13).

During the time that the child is in school, the school has virtually complete control over his everyday behavior. It tells him what and when he may eat, when and where he may relieve his bodily needs, even if both regulations force the child to deviate from nonschool patterns; it tells him what behavior is acceptable and what behavior is not. It also has the ability to carry this power outside the school setting by bringing in the parents and keeping records. The latter point has been made by Edgar Friedenberg who adds that the cumulative folders, as well as attendance and tardiness records kept by the school, are given to business and government agencies upon request. This means that not only is the child's behavior looped from one class to another and from one school to another, but it also follows him after he leaves school.

The processes which have been discussed so far have all dealt with entrance into elementary school, particularly kindergarten. Though the examples given by no means exhaust instances of total behavior on this level, they are sufficient to indicate that one of the primary purposes of the early elementary school is to mold the child into a member. As the child progresses through school, the total aspects increase rather than decrease. For one thing, the kindergarten child spends less time in school than do older children; for another, the parents are still considered supreme by the child. The influence of the school has not reached its peak. When the child enters junior high and high school, he discovers that his behavior and production rate are judged. This is not to say that evaluation does not go on in elementary school but only that it is not as extreme or overt. Whereas the child in elementary school is told that he will not do well in reading, the high school student is told that he will not get into college, that he will not graduate, or that he will not be able to get a job with the kind of recommendations that the school will have to give him.

James Bryant Conant has gone so far as to suggest that every high school student be given a plastic card which would list his grades, attendance, and so forth. This would merely make official what is now open practice: the use of the school as an information depository for business and government. Since the students know the school is used as a source of information (they are often told so by their teachers), it is no surprise that they rarely come to their teachers or counselors with serious emotional, ethical, or personal problems.

Not only does his record follow the student after he leaves school, but the school also can determine in large part the single most important factor in that record: the method of egress from the school taken by the student. If a student has either broken enough of the school's rules or broken the same one often enough he can be expelled or suspended. This process depends, of course, on the power of the parents to bring pressure or countersanctions upon the school. Regardless of the parental power or other extenuating circumstances, however, the school, like the mental hospital, has the power to enforce its regulations by threatening to withhold the proper egress papers.

Taking all these considerations together, we might at least tentatively call the school a *semitotal institution*. During the six hours a day that the child is in school, the influence exerted on the child is sufficient to force him to conform to the patterns prescribed by the school or accept the consequences: he is forced to become a member of the institution.

Gym class at N. Junior
Girls gym suits.
Parochial schools.

Characteristic 2: Courses of Action Open to Students

If the model of the total institution is to hold for our purposes, the students in the school should respond to the processes of deculturization and reculturization with one of the four courses of action mentioned by Goffman. The first course of action open to the student is that of *situational withdrawal*. The student, for one reason or another, does not accept the definition of the situation presented by the school; but rather than fighting it, he ignores it. For example, the gang leader who recognizes his own abilities to lead a gang but who is placed in a remedial class, may reject the concept that he is stupid or even that he is uneducated. He may merely withdraw from the sanctions of the school by indicating that he doesn't care what the school says about him and that the remedial class seems to be the easiest way to get out of school without doing any work and still get passing grades. What he has done is to negate the power of the school over him by refusing to recognize that anything which the school does to him or for him is of any significance to his life. This is the "sit out" as opposed to the "dropout": he merely sits out the time until he graduates. He neither causes anyone else any trouble nor does he allow the school to cause him any. This student may be irritating and unrewarding, but he is generally of little concern to the adult staff since he is conforming to the role of the "typical lazy remedial student."

There is, however, another type of withdrawn student. This is the student who has withdrawn due to a sense of failure. This student says, in effect, "Don't try to teach me anything; I'm too stupid." He appears listless and unaware of his surroundings, with the exception of the bell which signals the end of the period. Another distinguishing characteristic of this type of withdrawal is that the withdrawal may not extend to all subject matters; the withdrawn English student may be expressive in shop, on the athletic field, or in history class.

Another type of withdrawn student is the psychologically disturbed child. The role of the school in this form of withdrawal will be discussed in Chapter 14.

Intransigence is a more open attack upon the authority of the school or particular class. Here the student refuses to obey, openly flaunts, or simply breaks the rules of the school and dares anyone to take action. In some cases the student may recognize that he has greater power, perhaps through the power of his family, than does the school. At other times, he may wish to defy the school openly for personal reasons. One of the dangers here is that the student's occasional "sounding" (insults designed to be taken in a half-joking fashion to see how far he can go without punishment) may be taken as defiance.

Colonization may be the most common response by the student who feels he has nothing better to do than go to school. Here the student recognizes that the school has little to offer him in terms of basic desires and needs, but that it's better than walking the streets. The general attitude is "live and let live." Often such a student uses the school not for its manifest function of attaining knowledge but rather for a latent function such as social contact.

Conversion occurs when the student simply accepts the definition of his role as presented by the school. This is easier for some students than it is for others. For example, as Paul Goodman has pointed out, the school is a predominantly feminine, middle-class institution, and so females find it easier to accept the definition of the situation as presented by the school. If statistics regarding discipline are any indication, it would appear that more boys than girls are referred for disciplinary matters, and more lower-class students are referred than middle- or upper-middle-class students.

For heuristic reasons the four characteristic responses have been separated, but in actual practice pure types of reaction will be less common than will mixtures of some sort. Most students do not recognize that they are adopting a set of roles in the school, since many of the roles have become part of the societal expectation of the school and are adopted out of awareness. It must also be remembered, however, that regardless of the course of action taken by the student, he, like the inmate in a mental hospital, will attempt to keep part of himself inviolate. This will be particularly true of those students who come into conflict with the institution. This attempt to maintain individuality within the institutional structure makes up the underlife.

Characteristic 3: The Underlife

The purpose of the underlife is to enable the inmate to maintain portions of his own individuality in the face of the institution's power. The connotation of the underlife is that this is done through covert attacks on the institution for which the inmate cannot be punished. This gives him a double feeling of self-worth, since he has been able to break the institution's rules and at the same time "put one over on them" in that, if the attack is well-planned and well-executed, he will not be punished. For example, a student is sent to the office and arrives some 45 minutes later. When asked what took him so long, he replies that he had to go to the bathroom. He knows that it is a lie, and he knows that the administrator knows that it is a lie, but they both know that there is little or nothing that can be done about it. This is a reasonably simple form of underlife. It can be far more complex. The complexity of the specific act is in part determined by the amount of control exercised over the individual by the school. The greater the control, the more complex and in many cases bizarre the behavior will appear. For example, the student in the social adjustment class who is far more closely watched than is his counterpart in a regular class must resort to making strange noises or belching or the like in order to indicate his individuality in the face of the institution.

A pattern of underlife can become endemic in a school. A group of students may find a teacher who does not pay attention during tests. Both in order to show their disregard for the values held by the school and to get a good grade without studying, students of a particular group will see to it that they make up a majority of the class and then cheat in any way possible. If an out-group member of the class indicates displeasure, he is convinced through social pressure that he should hold his tongue and cheat with the rest of the class. Sometimes the brightest students in the class, who could obtain a good grade without cheating, will seem to cheat so that they will not be ostracized by the group. Though this endemic form of underlife may occur, individual acts, which may elicit support from the rest of the class in the form of sympathetic laughter, are more common.

Is the School a Total Institution?

Since the characteristics of the school meet the above criteria, is it a total institution? This depends upon the *permeability* of the school. Permeability refers to the amount of cross-contact between the larger culture and the institution. Certainly the school is a far more permeable institution than is the mental hospital, but the Armed Forces are more permeable than the mental hospital too. The problem here is to determine whether there is so much cross-contact that it does not make sense to call the school a total institution at all. One example of cross-contact is the encouragement parents are given to take an interest in the school and the welfare of their child within that school. Parents are urged to join the PTA, and in some cases pressure may be brought to bear upon the child if his parents are not members of the PTA. If we look more closely at the relationship between parent and school, however, we see that there is not nearly the permeability we may have originally suspected. It is almost impossible for a parent to "just look around" the school. There are particular times when parents are allowed to enter the school, talk to teachers, and review their child's work. Open houses, PTA meetings, and father's nights are examples. Viewed from the standpoint of the school as a total institution, the purpose of these gatherings is not to make the school more permeable, but rather to make it less permeable while seeming to make it more so. If a parent has a complaint or just wants to learn more about the school, he is told to become active in the PTA or a similar organization. If he becomes active, he may feel that

he is getting close to the school. But if he analyzes the school personnel with whom he has come into contact, he will soon realize that he has spoken only to the principal or to the faculty PTA representative, who often has been appointed by the principal. If there were no PTA or father's nights, any interested parent could go to the school and talk to the people involved. If this occurred, the school would be open to the public. We are not interested in the value of the open school at this time; we merely conclude that the PTA and other such devices are subsidiary organizations which are designed to keep parents and the public from directly intervening in the school. This may not be the intended manifest function of the PTA, but it is a latent actual function.

When we combine all the factors, it seems feasible to assume that the school bears a sufficient similarity to other total institutions so that the construct of the total institution has some validity. This construct is basic to the theoretical formulation of this book. Without the construct of the power of the school over the individual, for example, it does not make sense to talk about the role of the school in mental health or juvenile delinquency. An intrinsic part of the role of the school is that it does have power over the behavior of the child in the present and in the future. The school does change the behavior of the child from whatever it was before he entered school to a behavior which conforms to the value structure of the school; it does attempt to change the nonmember to the member.

Whether this attempt is good or bad will be determined in large part by what is considered good or bad by the society. If the society is particularly interested in academic achievement and is technologically oriented, then the main purpose of the school is to impart knowledge to the young. This can be accomplished most efficiently if all the students are quiet, if there is homogeneous grouping of students on the basis of academic ability, if there are negative sanctions for failure, and so forth. In this type of society, the more total the school, the better. On the other hand, if the school strives to teach independence of thought and action rather than technology, then the school will allow as much freedom as possible to individual students, there will be little if any homogeneous grouping, and there will be fewer sanctions for failure in academic classes. The purposes of these two schools are quite different, so the method of training children is quite different. Correspondingly, the role expectations for the children are different.

Thus whether the school is viewed as oppressive and total is determined in large part by the viewpoint of the parents and the children. If the community is academically oriented, the school will appear to be less total and autocratic than would the same school in a non-academically oriented community. The construct of the school as a total institution may not answer the question "What do we do to children?" but it does give one method for analyzing "How do we do it?"

BIBLIOGRAPHY

Friedan, Betty, *The Feminine Mystique*, Norton, New York, 1963.

Friedenberg, Edgar Z., *The Vanishing Adolescent*, Dell, New York, 1959.

Goffman, Erving, *Presentations of Self in Everyday Life*, Doubleday, Anchor Books, Garden City, N.Y. 1959.

Goffman, Erving, *Asylums*, Doubleday, Anchor Books, Garden City, N.Y., 1961.

Goodman, Paul, *Growing Up Absurd*, Random House, New York, 1956.

Scheff, Thomas J., "The Role of the Mentally Ill and the Dynamics of Mental Disorder," *Sociometry*, 1963, vol. 26, no. 4, 436–453.

Shanley, Fred, Jalil Alzobaire, and D. Welty Lefever, "Comparative Analysis of School and Behavioral Data for Aggressive, Well-Adjusted, and Underachieving Students," Youth Studies Center, University of Southern California, Los Angeles, 1964.

Chapter 7 / *The School as a Culture*

The previous three chapters dealt with the school as an institution; this chapter, based largely on Edward T. Hall's *The Silent Language* views the school as a culture. Hall stresses the need to understand the way unfamiliar cultures handle modes of interaction. He believes that much of the conflict and difficulty that arise between groups occurs because each does not understand how the other handles interaction patterns. With this in mind, he suggests specific methods which can be used to ease conflict situations by analyzing and understanding the handling of these interaction patterns.

The purpose in this chapter, of course, is not so much to understand a foreign culture as to understand a culture which may be less different but still different enough so that conflict exists. Specifically, the differences to which we refer are between the adult school culture and the student school culture, lower-class culture and middle-class culture, and minority-group culture and majority-group culture. Our goal is to present a method of analysis for these cultures so that varying patterns may be recognized and understood.

Three Reaction Patterns

According to Hall, there are three general types of interaction patterns within a society: formal, informal, and technical patterns. *Formal* patterns are those behaviors performed for traditional reasons. The individual rarely questions their rationale: "Theirs not to reason why, theirs but to do and die." *Informal* patterns of behavior are those of which the individual generally is unconscious. For example, we learn to speak by imitation. There is often no conscious effort in learning to speak; we simply imitate those around us and thereby learn the sounds common to our culture. Most of the significant learnings of children occur in this fashion. Speech, walking, running, many of the games children play, and basic interaction patterns with peers are all learned in this out-of-awareness fashion. Rarely, if ever, is a child formally taught these patterns.

Technical patterns are distinguishable from both the formal and the informal patterns in that the individual practicing the pattern is fully aware of how he learned it, why he learned it, and why he is performing the behavior. For example, though a child learns to talk informally, he learns to use the telephone technically; that is, he must be taught which end to speak into and which end to listen to. He is taught that it is possible to speak to people even when you cannot see them and when they are at a great distance from the speaker. Speaking on the telephone, then, is a technical pattern.

The Primary Message Systems

Within these three types of patterns, Hall bases his analysis on the *primary message systems*. It is Hall's contention that if an individual learns ten primary message systems and understands the way in which a particular culture deals with each, he will then be able to understand the culture fully and completely and thereby live in harmony with it. The ten primary message systems are interaction, association, subsistence, bisexuality, territoriality, temporality, learning, play, defense, and exploitation. Thus, if a teacher enters a classroom and understands the way in which the children have learned to interact, the way they associate with one another, their humor or play, their bisexual patterns, and so forth, then he will be able to understand and communicate with the children without conflict. If, on the other hand, the teacher does not understand the way in which the children handle these various cultural patterns, and if they do not understand him, then the probabilities are much greater that there will be difficulty and conflict between the teacher and students. It is, therefore, of paramount importance that teachers learn a method of analyzing the cultural situation in which they find themselves. Let us examine each of the primary message systems individually to see how this interplay among behavioral patterns within our culture works.

Each of the ten primary message systems can be seen from one of the three standpoints discussed above; that is, each primary message system can be either formal, informal, or technical. It should not be assumed that societies or message systems fall neatly into one or another of the categories, however, since few societies are either all formal, all informal, or all technical. It is possible for a society to deal with one message system formally, another informally, and a third technically. It is also possible for a society to deal with a particular message system formally in one situation, informally in another, and technically in a third. For example, a child may speak technically into the telephone, informally with his friends, and formally with adult authority figures such as teachers.

INTERACTION

The first of the primary message systems, *interaction*, refers to the general way in which people or groups of people or institutions relate to one another. Formal patterns of interaction are exemplified by such times and places as China in the time of Confucius. In China at that time patterns of interaction were highly formalized, and everyone knew exactly what his role was and how this role related to the others in his institutions and society. A father knew exactly what his relation to his wife and children was, and the children knew exactly what their relation was to their parents. In each case, the role was highly formalized and traditional, and there was little if any deviation from it. Although no society is entirely formal, informal, or technical, Confucianist China was certainly an example of a society which was largely formalized.

An example of informal interaction would be the way in which children tend to interact on their first day in a classroom. Although there are some formal patterns which can be seen immediately by an observer, such as boys sitting near other boys and girls sitting near other girls, by and large the patterns are informal; that is, children sit largely where they find it most convenient to sit. It is only after the teacher has arrived in the room and placed them in alphabetical order, all facing forward and ready to learn, that a technical or formal pattern appears.

One of the significant characteristics of modern United States culture is that it is highly technical. According to Marshall McLuhan one of the reasons Americans tend to interact the way they do is because of the technical features involved in the interaction process: the telephone, television, newspapers, letters, and other means of communication. Even very young children learn that it is sometimes more convenient to communicate with friends or acquaintances over the telephone than in the face-to-face situation of street discussion since the latter involves going outside or going to the person's home. Children in our society often learn to interact technically, that is via technical means of one sort or another rather than informally or formally.

Furthermore, our technical society has enabled us to become highly mobile geographically. This has its effect on interaction patterns; it is so common to move from one place to another that friendships must be developed which can be broken on relatively short notice. In this way more transitory friendships are developed. Correspondingly, whereas in nontechnical societies it is important to be able to get along with one's immediate neighbors, in the highly technical society, with its freeways, thruways, and mass transit, it is not particularly important, since one's friends and one's neighbors may be entirely different groups of people.

Interaction problems often occur when one person expects one pattern of interaction and another person expects another. For example, if a child knows a particular teacher in an informal nonschool pattern, it is difficult for the child to shift into the formal school pattern. If a teacher is also a relative, it is difficult for the child to shift from "Aunt Sarah" to "Miss Jones," even though this shift from informal to formal is necessitated by the change in situation. Under these circumstances conflict can occur. In this particular example, of course, the conflict is relatively easily settled. In other situations, however, it might not be so easily handled. For example, when the child's pattern of interaction is one which the teacher generally considers to be far too informal, while on the other hand the teacher's pattern of interaction is one which the child considers far too formal, conflict will occur. The child expects the teacher to accept joking behavior, a certain amount of physical body contact, and so forth, while the teacher demands respect, no body contact, and generally a more formal recognition of role differentiation. Unless one or the other is willing to change his pattern of interaction, the distinction between the formal and informal will continue to be a source of conflict between teacher and student.

ASSOCIATION

The second primary message system is *association*, the order or organization of the society and of its various parts. As with interaction, association falls into three primary patterns: formal, informal, and technical. The animal world abounds in formal association patterns. For example, wolves travel in packs and have leaders, scouts, hunters, and protectors. The same is true of orangutans and, to some extent, chimpanzees. Chickens have a formal pecking order; that is, the leader of the flock of chickens can peck the number-two chicken out of the way. The second-status chicken then pecks the number-three chicken and so on down to the last and weakest chicken who is the last to get any of the food. This is an example of formal organization.

The same kind of formal organizations occur in human institutions, particularly highly formalized institutions such as the Army or the school. In the Army, the formal organization is from general down to private. In the school, the formal organization is from the superintendent or chief school officer down to the student. Even though the general may not be smarter or better equipped to administrate than the private, and the school superintendent may be no better than the student, this organization has been maintained and is the formal pattern.

An informal pattern of association within the animal world exists with jackals. Jackals tend not to travel in packs; they come together to hunt, kill the hunted animal, eat it without any formal pattern as to who eats first or last, and then separate and go their own way. The same thing happens with people who stop at a bus stop to catch the same bus, or ride the same train into the city day in and day out. Initially the patterns are informal, though the people waiting at the bus stop and the people catching the train may develop more formal organization as time goes on. They have come together with the same purpose, but not in order to meet with one another.

Technical patterns of association are of course more rare in the animal world, though on occasion even animals are forced into living on a technical basis. An example of this would be animals (or men!) who are forced to live on reservations due to the technical advances of the people around them in which they either cannot or will not take part.

Possibly the best example of a technical pattern of association is urban life. Though urban life has developed some formal patterns of association (such as the habit of people who live in apartment houses not to speak to their immediate neighbors, so as to maintain some semblance of privacy), by and large the pattern of urban dwellers is a technical one; that is, people come together not because of a pattern handed down from their ancestors or because they happen to fall together in one place, but because it is technically more convenient to live in a city close to where one works and interacts. Part of this technical pattern of association is that it is possible to segregate audiences. The audience or people with whom we perform one type of associate activity is not the same as those with whom we perform another type. For example, those people with whom we work are often not the same people with whom we associate socially. There are certain advantages in that the individual is not expected to maintain the same role or degree of role stability from one situation to the next. On the other hand, it is a disadvantage in that the individual does not develop strong loyalties to either his social associates or his work associates.

SUBSISTENCE

The third primary message system relates to the way people handle *subsistence*, that is, eating habits, employment, and the patterns needed to subsist in society. In formal subsistence patterns, religious practices are often connected with the planting of crops, the consumption of food, and so forth. In many societies there are still both planting and harvesting feasts as well as prayers or grace at meals. These are formal patterns. Some of them are performed out of habit, without the people who are directly involved knowing their original purpose.

Many city dwellers tend to deal with subsistence patterns in an informal fashion; that is, subsistence is on a catch-as-catch-can basis. There is no set time for eating meals, there is no particular place where meals are eaten, and there are no definite people with whom meals are eaten. To the modern urban dweller, subsistence becomes a subsidiary pattern. With whom he eats, with whom he works, and what the employment is becomes less important than the fact that he has a job and that he can find a place to eat.

This informality of subsistence may also be related directly to the technical aspects of subsistence within a modern industrial society. For instance, in modern industrial society it is no longer a great chore for the wife to cook reasonably palatable meals. She can go to the freezer and prepare a full-fledged meal in a half-hour. The husband, if he so chooses, can stop for a meal at an automat where there is little concern either for him as an individual or for his culinary habits. He is simply an object to be fed, and what is placed before him is an object to be eaten. Whether what he eats is particularly palatable is almost beside the point, since his purpose is to eat as quickly and as efficiently as he can so that he can get back to the business at hand. The technical pattern tends to lower the importance of the particular subsistence or employment.

BISEXUALITY

Bisexuality relates to the way in which males and females treat one another. In formal patterns of bisexuality, the two individuals involved have less choice over their own behavior. To a large extent the traditions of the society determine what their behavior will be. Weddings are arranged; premarital relations either exist or do not exist as the society dictates; bisexual patterns between two persons often are the concern of the extended family, and in some cases the entire community; and the relationship between husband and wife will be largely determined by the societal decisions.

Formal patterns of bisexuality stand in opposition to the informal pattern in which there are few if any formalized or traditional rules and regulations. Modern United States bisexual behavior is a good example of this, since the formal patterns of arranged marriages and codes of ethics regarding premarital and extramarital sexual behavior have broken down. There is a more informal pattern in which each individual or couple can determine his own behavior.

Again, as with other primary message systems, there is a direct interaction between the informal and the technical patterns of bisexual behavior. There is good reason to believe that one of the reasons for the informality of bisexual patterns in the United States during the 1950s and 1960s is the technical advances with regard to contraception. With technical advances there has been an increase in marriages of convenience, marriages without children, and even trial marriages. The greatest single technical influence on bisexual behavior has been the increase in reasonably sure and safe contraception. This has taken the primary stigma and fear of pregnancy from premarital and postmarital sexual behavior and has changed the entire sequence of events leading to courtship and marriage, as well as many of the marital and extramarital sexual patterns.

TERRITORIALITY

Territoriality refers not only to the way in which a society handles landrights, but also to the way in which it handles all property rights. For example, some native African societies have no sense of personal property at all since they have no concept of formal property rights. All things are held in common. Some societies, such as most Western cultures, tend to believe that property rights are extremely important—"A man's home is his castle." Examples of formal patterns of territoriality would be such things as the divine right of Kings and the primacy of law, both written and unwritten. Informal patterns, on the other hand, would include "finders keepers," or "possession is nine-tenths of the law"; within the informal pattern, boundaries tend to be fluid and ill-defined. Within the technical pattern of territoriality there is some reliance on the technical, as opposed to formal, patterns of the law, but there is an even greater reliance on sheer power; he who has the greatest power will maintain the greatest amount of territory.

The school aids greatly in teaching children the importance of looking at property and territory formally and technically. When the child is in school he is taught to respect the property of others and of the school and to maintain his property rights over his own possessions. Everything within the school belongs specifically to someone. Even his own performance in academic areas and citizenship is his alone; it does not belong to the entire class. A child may fail in either citizenship or in his academic studies, and if he does so it is his responsibility alone.

In other cultures, such as the Soviet Union, if a child fails either in citizenship or in academic areas, it becomes the concern of the entire class. If any person fails, it is the responsibility and the shame of the entire class since the class is a communal unit. For this reason, the Soviet Union attempts to see to it that every person passes every subject; the emphasis is upon communal rather than on individual being.

TEMPORALITY

A relatively easy message system to diagnose, and one of the most important to the school, is *temporality* or time. One of the serious difficulties facing many schools is that although the school tends to handle time very technically (school begins at 9:00, not 9:05 or 8:55), the students may handle time quite informally. For example, the Navajo or Hopi Indians of the American Southwest tend to handle time extremely informally. Things begin when they are ready to begin, and not before and not after. This may mean that school will open at 10:15 one day, 9:00 another, and not at all on a third day.

It is the conflict between various patterns of temporality which makes the school difficult for children at first, since they must learn a technical method of handling time. To some extent they have, of course, learned these patterns at home through having to be home for dinner on time, but the definition of "on time" is different at home. At home there is a leeway of a certain number of minutes or even hours, depending on the particular pattern within the home; at school there is very little leeway within the "on time" system. One of the more common reasons for expulsion or suspension is not that the student is absent but that the student tends to be late. Because neither the school nor the student recognizes that there is a conflict in culture, the conflict is not understood and remains unresolved until the less powerful of the two parties involved, the student, either changes or is eliminated through suspension or expulsion. To resolve the conflict, understanding of the pattern is needed; then the school, the child, or perhaps even both can change.

Formal patterns of temporality deal again with traditional methods of handling time. For example, the English custom of having tea at 4:00 regardless of the circumstances is a formal pattern. Whether or not it makes sense to have tea at 4:00 in the middle of the Arabian desert is a moot point; in any case, the formal pattern persists. The same is true of temporal patterns of sleeping. Whether it makes any particular sense for an individual to work during the daytime and sleep at night in a modern urban setting is again disputable. For an artist who needs the natural sunlight, obviously the daylight hours are extremely important; but for a writer who needs quiet and solitude, the night may be a far more convenient time in which to work. The writer will, however, be forced into a daytime life to some degree, simply because the rest of the society, through a traditional, formal pattern, uses the day to work and the night to sleep.

LEARNING

Learning also differs greatly in terms of formal, informal, and technical patterns. An example of a formal pattern of learning is the traditional didactic approach: the student is given a recitation to learn, recites it, and is graded on his work. There is very little interchange, but there is a highly formal pattern. The rules and regulations for teacher behavior, such as maintaining a distance between student and teacher because "familiarity breeds contempt" or "the quiet classroom is a good classroom" are part of this formal pattern. Whether there is any demonstrable relationship between neatness, quiet, or distance and good teaching is questionable, but the formal tradition connects these norms of learning with good teaching.

Whereas the school has many formal patterns of learning, the child has learned largely through informal patterns; that is, through imitation and "learning by doing." For instance, the child learns language not by being systematically taught how to speak, but by listening to those around him and finding that it is more convenient to ask for the milk than it is to shout or mumble something incomprehensible. He also learns how to play with his peers, he learns about nature—he learns all those things necessary in order to interact, associate, or play adequately in a society. No one specifically teaches the child these things; he learns them through observation and emulation. When the child enters school, however, he is in effect told that he must change his pattern of learning from an informal one to a formal one. The first job of the school, then, is to change his pattern of learning. This immediately means that there will be a conflict between the child and the school until the child has changed his patterns from the informal to the formal.

There has also been a great increase in technical patterns within the school with the increase in teaching machines, programed text books, and so forth. Again the technical pattern has great influence on the informal and the formal patterns; teaching machines certainly affect the interaction between student and teacher. In most cases, the manifest reason for including teaching machines is to give the teacher more time to deal directly with the student and become more familiar with his individual academic problems. Such machines are often used, however, as a method for eliminating an aspect of teacher-student response; the teaching machine or the programed textbook has been placed between the teacher and the student so that the teacher does not need to communicate with the child. Again the problem is one of conflict in pattern. The important thing to remember is that differential patterns do exist, do cause conflict, and are usually resolved by the submission of the individual to the greater power of the institution.

PLAY

The eighth primary message system deals with the way in which people *play* or entertain themselves. An example of a formal pattern is much of the play or entertainment of the

Orient, such as flower arranging or forms of karate and jujitsu. All have a very definite formal philosophical base as well as an entertainment base. Informal patterns of play are those largely adopted by children in Western culture, such as sand-lot ball games, making sled runs out of a convenient hill, or choosing teams on the basis of who happens to arrive at what time rather than on the basis of necessary skill.

Technical patterns of play include such things as Little League baseball, where the informal sand-lot game has become a highly structured team sport with a great deal of competition both for the children and for the parents. Spectator sports also fall into this general category of technical play. Since we are a largely technical society, we tend to engage in technical kinds of sports, mostly team sports. Unfortunately, much of the sports activity which we teach in the school is of little value to the individual when he leaves the school, since technical spectator sports are learned in school and yet the informal active sports are more usable in adult life.

DEFENSE

The ninth primary message system is *defense*. One of the most common formal patterns of defense is religion. Religion is used in a traditional sense to defend us from storms, the attacks of enemies, or even death. An example of informal defense is the citizen soldier, traditionally the minuteman of the United States, who is not a soldier in his everyday life but becomes a soldier at those times when he or his country feels that he is needed. Technical patterns of defense include weapons such as today's guided missiles and atomic bombs .

Difficulty occurs in the school situation with regard to some of the formal and informal patterns of defense. For instance, in some schools students have many formal patterns of defense and offense which the school may or may not recognize. The boy whose mother is called a name may feel that he has been directly attacked and therefore must defend himself. If he does not defend himself, he will be considered a coward and will be subject to constant future attacks. He therefore physically attacks the person who has blasphemed his mother. This is a formal pattern, recognized by children for centuries. On the other hand, the school, which also has its formal patterns, does not recognize the students' formal pattern of defense as being legitimate and says, in effect, that verbal attacks cannot be answered by physical attacks. Therefore the student who engages in this behavior must be suspended or expelled. In this particular example, the conflict is not so much between different types of patterns as between different definitions of formal patterns.

EXPLOITATION

The last of the primary message systems is *exploitation.* Formal exploitation again has its basis in tradition, law, or veneration. For example, there are a number of legal means whereby individuals can exploit one another within American society. A particularly vivid example of this is the small loan in which it is perfectly legal to charge 20, 30, or even 40 percent annual interest. This has been formalized in law and in tradition and has become almost accepted within the American framework. Only recently has the lender even been required to state how much annual interest he is charging. Another example would be the sexual behavior of the American male, who traditionally is expected to exploit his female counterpart to the greatest extent possible. The American male who wishes to marry a virgin but to have intercourse with as many eligible females as possible previous to his marriage, exemplifies this type of exploitation. Indeed, in many aspects of life, it has become almost a formal pattern within the American society to get as much as possible from others and at the same time give as little as possible of oneself.

There is also a good deal of informal exploitation—exploitation which is largely unintentional. For example, the Southern plantation owners who planted cotton and then, when the land was depleted, moved on to new fields, burned off the trees, and again planted cotton; who again depleted the fields and again moved on were not systematically exploiting the land. In many cases they did not realize what they were doing to the land; theirs was a more informal, unconscious pattern of exploitation.

Technical patterns of exploitation have been the most common within the United States. As the United States has become more technically oriented, it has exploited its natural resources and its people on a technical level. One example of this is the individual who works on an assembly line, and does the same thing day in and day out. His work is dreary, yet he must continue it if he wishes to continue being paid. In this case a human being has been exploited for the sake of technical efficiency.

United States society also has exploited and continues to exploit natural resources. Redwood trees are felled so that man may use the wood even though it may take 3000 years to grow a redwood tree. Major canyons, such as the Glenn Canyon, are partially destroyed to build dams for electric power. The conflict here involves a balance of power between conservation and technical exploitation. This is not to say that technical exploitation is not necessary; the point is that where some other societies might have greater respect for nature, and thereby might exploit it in a far more understanding fashion, the United States traditionally has exploited its natural resources without thought to the future.

The Interplay of the Systems in the Schools

Table 4 has been prepared in order to make the primary message systems more meaningful. Several of the most important message systems have been used to indicate how the administration, teachers, and students handle selected primary message systems.

The administration handles interaction and association in a highly formal fashion; it maintains a distance from students and faculty, and relies heavily on rules and regulations. The

TABLE 4

Patterns of Heading Four Primary Message Systems

Primary Message System	Administrative Pattern	Teacher Pattern	Student Pattern
Interaction and association	Highly formal	Somewhat informal	Informal
Subsistence	Technical and informal	Technical and informal	Informal
Bisexuality	Technical	Technical and formal	Informal-exploratory or formal ("going steady")
Temporality	Technical	Technical	Technical-curricular or informal-extracurricular

teacher tends to be somewhat informal with both the administrator and the student; he tends to speak less in terms of rules, regulations, and traditions. The students, on the other hand, relate to one another in a far more informal and technical fashion; their interactions and associations are based largely on who sits next to them in class, who walks to and from school with them, and who shares their common interests. The one formal pattern which does exist within student culture is that associations tend to fall along socioeconomic status lines. This is largely due to parental and peer pressure.

Subsistence can be defined as "making it" in school, or the ability of the student to pass courses and get out. The administrator tends to define subsistence in technical and informal patterns. The technical pattern is based largely on his role as grade-giver, diploma-giver, and disciplinarian. The informal pattern is based largely on the pressure and influence of the community; those parents who have great influence within the community will be able to exert pressure on the decisions, whereas those parents who have little or no influence in the the community will not.

Teachers also tend to deal with subsistence on a technical and informal level. They are also governed in part both by their roles as teachers in terms of grades and discipline and the informal pressures of the community. Because of their closeness to the students, however, they are also governed by an informal pattern of likes and dislikes.

Students, on the other hand, are far more governed by their informal patterns. They are not particularly interested in the technical patterns of grades or discipline; they are far more interested in the informal pattern of their social leaders. In a number of studies conducted by the author, when teachers were asked to indicate the leaders in a class, they almost always chose the academic work leaders. When the students were asked to pick the leaders, they almost always picked the social leaders. The patterns among students are far more informal than they are among teachers and administrators.

Bisexuality is also dealt with in different ways by administrators, teachers, and students. The administrator tends to deal with bisexuality in a highly formal technical fashion. In the United States today, the administrator deals with bisexuality by telling the students that "bisexual behavior is not acceptable in school." This bisexual behavior may be defined as holding hands, walking together down the halls, sitting together in classrooms, or actual sexual relations. Whatever the definition, it should be remembered that the principal's primary interest here is maintenance of order and absence of scandal and publicity. He is not primarily a teacher of morals; he is a technician.

The teacher, on the other hand, is not only a technician but also a teacher of morals. That is, the teacher is not only required to say that under no circumstances should bisexual behavior be allowed in school, but he is also expected to say that bisexual behavior previous to marriage (meaning here actual sexual relations) is not acceptable under any circumstances in the society at large. Students have a number of sexual patterns which they follow at various times; one is an informal exploratory and exploitive pattern in which both male and female attempt to find out as much as they can about bisexual relations without endangering themselves, and in some cases with little concern for the danger of their partner. There are also a number of formal patterns in bisexual behavior such as going steady or being pinned. Another formal pattern which is expected of students by the parents and by the school is that of chastity. As mentioned before, however, a number of technical patterns which have come into play during the last 10 to 15 years may be changing the formal pattern of chastity. Two of these are contraceptives, which make sexual relations "safer," and the automobile, which enables the children to get away from their parents and the school. The students, then, may have quite a different set of rules within their own group than those put forth by administrators, teachers, or even parents.

In terms of temporality, the administration and the teachers both handle time in a highly technical fashion. It is precise; it is exact; and breaking the temporal rules carries many negative sanctions. The students, on the other hand, have to maintain two patterns. One is the technical pattern which they have learned in school in order to function within the school, and the other is the informal extracurricular pattern which has a great deal more leeway and involves their peers.

Summary

In this chapter, an attempt has been made to present another method of analysis for the study of the school. The particular system used here has been Edward T. Hall's study of culture. Hall's concept of the primary message systems has been used for the specific analysis of culture and of the school as a setting for cultural conflict.

BIBLIOGRAPHY

Hall, Edward T., *The Silent Language*, Fawcett, Premier Books, Greenwich, Conn., 1959.

McLuhan, Marshall, *Understanding Media*, McGraw-Hill, New York, 1964.

PART III

THE SCHOOL IN SOCIAL PERSPECTIVE

Part III presents a view of the school in its social environment. The models provided in Part II are analytical tools—conceptual in nature, theoretical in orientation, but practical as devices for comprehending education. The reader is encouraged to experiment with these models, to test their value, and to develop an increasingly analytical approach to the study of education as he applies them to the topics of Parts III and IV.

There is a tendency today to view schools in mechanistic terms: to study how many students and how many teachers there are, how their time is divided, how they read books, how they comb their hair, what subjects they enjoy and detest, and so forth. This is no disparagement of the need for accurate data about schools; indeed adequate analysis requires sound data. But it is easier to acquire than to analyze and apply data. For this reason, we have supplied the necessary analytical tools before discussing data and concrete examples.

Because most readers have had considerable experience with schools in one form or another but have not had common experiences nor analytical opportunities, the following view of the school in social perspective should be somewhat illuminating. It provides some data about American education and American society, some interpretations of the data, and some commentary on the relation of the school to society. This material can be used both as a background and as a framework for analyzing particular schools.

Chapter 8 is an overview of social structure and of population dynamics as they relate to education. Chapter 9 discusses the socioeconomic factors of social class, caste, and mobility. Chapter 10 focuses directly on the structure and function of education in America, and Chapter 11 deals with individuals and dysfunctional elements in the social psychology of schools. Finally, Chapter 12 presents a view of the teacher in American society, social and school roles, and conflicts.

Chapter 8 / *Social Structure and Population*

As indicated earlier, education is a socially contrived institution which has direct and indirect links to its society. It has social power and social responsibility. *Social power* refers to the influence of the school over its pupils and alumni, and *social responsibility* is the influence that the society has over the nature of education. Education is not socially sterile; on the contrary, it is dynamic and changes with society.

Arguments over the purposes of education in a society are basically arguments over the hypothetical nature of a society. If one maintains that the schools should be more selective in admission of students (an elitist position), he is really proposing a value system for the society based upon whatever criteria he selects for admission or continuance in schools. That is, if admission to secondary or higher education is limited to those of sufficient wealth or social position, as has been true in American educational history, then the criteria of wealth and position are given high priority in the value system of the society. If the criterion is intellectual prowess, then intellectualism is given high priority in the society. Even if schooling is open to all, there is a system of priorities; here equality is of high priority. In each case, the purposes of education are closely tied to the structure of society.

When the curriculum is considered, arguments over what knowledge is of most worth tend to be arguments related to the social as well as intellectual worth of any particular knowledge. The Latin Grammar Schools, the first secondary schools in the American colonies, limited enrollment and offered course work for entrance to higher education and ministerial and social-leadership positions. Courses were conducted in Latin, and classical studies were stressed. With the development of less stringent requirements of social class, the evolution of rugged individualism, the emergence of equalitarian ideas, the economic needs of the budding industrial revolution, and the opportunities for exploration and settlement of the frontiers, the American schools became less concerned with admissions restricted by wealth and status, more concerned with applied and scientific studies, and more related to the entire society.

The movement to mass education, which is now entrenched in the United States, is becoming an international phenomenon. European countries that in the past had prided themselves on the high quality of secondary schools resulting from their elite admissions and stiff academic curricula are now developing institutions comparable to the American comprehensive high school. These new schools have open admissions policies and a variety of curricula. In the United States the mass education movement is now reaching higher education through such avenues as the G.I. Bill, junior colleges without tuition, state-funded public colleges and universities, and extension and correspondence offerings.

Thus American history clearly indicates that schools and society are linked and that major activities of the school or society have an impact on each other. The questions of school admissions and of broadness of curricula are aspects of the relation of school to society which relate to social class, caste, status, stratification, and mobility. The structure and operation of both mass and elite educational systems have an influence on and are influenced by the structures of society.

A modern society has many components, but it is dangerous to make lists of categories which are presumed to incorporate all aspects of anything as dynamic as society. Societies are greater than the sum of their parts. Consequently, we will deal only with the factors in the social structure which are deemed most important to education. For the purposes of viewing education in American society, these factors include population trends and distribution, social caste and class, and social mobility. Since American schools involve people in a variety of ways according to age, sex, race, location, culturally rated intelligence, group size, and social status, we shall begin with these factors and the way that they relate to the educational institutions of today.

Population Dynamics

Education, like society as a whole, is directly affected by increases or decreases in and distribution of population. There are several areas of education in which this relationship to population is particularly evident.

ECONOMIC IMPACT

As population increases, there is a need for either increased educational facilities or for a social decision to limit admissions to schools. If the population increment is composed mainly of children, this may have a serious economic impact on communities and the society. Thus the drop in birth rate experienced during the depressions lowered the economic pressure on education, while the jump in birth rate after World War II has raised educational expense considerably. The stabilized birth rate, which is a current phenomenon, will result in some slowing of expense increases in schools, but the postwar baby boom is still exerting pressure on colleges. Also the overall cost of education per pupil increases as more and more students continue on to higher education.

URBANIZATION

The process of urbanization has been going on for some time in the United States. Indeed today there is a trend toward *suburbanization* and *metropolitanization.* When the population was distributed in rural areas with wide expanses of space, schools developed as small, discrete units varying in size, curriculum, quality, expense, and purpose according to their community. As urban population centers arose and the economy of the city became important, city school districts emerged. The institutional structure of education began to include large bureaucracies, common programs for students, and major tax investments. Then as the flight to the suburbs developed, taking from the cities the tax resources of the urban middle class, the city schools were altered considerably and the suburban school district with homogeneous students and values developed. The implications for education of the present shift toward metropolitan or megalopolitan populations are still unfolding.

TECHNOLOGY

Population seems to be in close relation to the state of technology in a society. It would be difficult to state a definite causal relationship between the two, but we do know that advances in technology affect the growth and distribution of population. Improved farming, mechanical conveniences, transportation and communications improvements, and the developing technologies related to space and electronics have had substantial influence on the development of urban and suburban populations. Medical technology has an obvious relation to birth and death rates and a subsequent impact on population trends.

Technological advances and their corollaries for population

are directly related to education. The needs of a technological society include production of technicians and scientists in addition to increased technical literacy of the general public. Thus American schools offer increasing amounts of work in technical subjects, some of which were unknown a few decades ago. Junior colleges offer programs for many technological careers, including training for dental, medical, data-processing, engineering, and electronics technicians. As technology continues to free the population from physical labors, there is an increasing need for technically educated, skilled employees and a decreasing need for unskilled labor.

Improved technology also has a utilitarian value to education. Television, programed teaching machines, computers, and other devices born in a period of technological growth have altered the potentials of education. It is now technically possible to provide education of a high quality at any number of locations simultaneously. Students may see and hear outstanding persons and events at home, on a bus, in a factory, at a pool hall, or in a cubicle in the library. Instantaneous transmission of learning materials to any geographical region is feasible; thus most of the world watched when men landed on the moon. It is also technically possible to provide separate, unique learning experiences for each student based on his own interests, abilities, motivations, and weaknesses. On the negative side, it is equally possible to dehumanize the educational process by technically abolishing the need for interpersonal relations in a classroom, gymnasium, school hallway, or boiler room. Technology can overcome the worst and destroy the best in an educational system; it can also leave a duly punched student marked "do not bend, fold, staple, or mutilate."

Population Growth and Composition

The population of the world has increased approximately sixfold since 1650. By the year 2000, given the current rate of increase, the world population will total over 6 billion people, compared to an estimated 3½ billion people at this time.

Homo habilis (the earliest man uncovered so far) was carbon-dated, and his period on earth was found to be about 1¾ to 2 million years ago. From this time to the birth of Christ, the population grew to about 250 million people. That is, it took well over 1 million years to reach a population of 250 million. It took another 1600 years to add another 250 million to the population of the earth. Only 200 years more (1650 to 1850) were needed to double the population again. In the twentieth century it required only 11 years, 1950 to 1961, to increase the population by another 500 million people.

The increase in population growth is a ratio between birth and death. Obviously, if births and deaths are equal, there is no population growth; and equally obviously there has been a considerable increase in the rate of growth recently. In 1945 the rate of world population growth was about 1 percent per year. In the 1960s this world rate reached almost 2 percent per year, or enough to double the population each 35 years. In the United States the growth rate is relatively low, but still averages between 1 percent and 1½ percent per year. If this rate were to remain constant for the next 100 years, the present estimated U.S. population of 200 million would increase to over 1 billion. Men born in America this year will probably live in a United States twice as densely populated as it is today by the time they retire.[1] This growth factor is shown in Table 5.

The estimated total population of the U.S. exceeded 200 million by 1969. Despite this size, the present growth rate is lower than any period since 1940. This is mainly the result of a decrease in birth rate—now the lowest of any period in the records of the country. Annual birth rates have continued downward since the peak years of the 1950s, while death rates have stabilized at about 9.5 per thousand population. Although the rate of civilian immigration is low in comparison with birth rates, immigration is contributing to a larger proportion of net growth now than at any time in recent history. This is the result of a decreasing birth rate while

TABLE 5

U.S. Population Growth Rates, 1935–1968[a]

Year	Birth Rate	Death Rate	Immigration Rate[b]	Net Growth Rate	Percent Growth Rate
1968	17.4	9.6	2.2	10.0	1.0
1967	17.8	9.3	2.2	10.7	1.1
1966	18.5	9.5	2.4	11.5	1.2
1965	19.5	9.4	2.0	12.2	1.2
1962	22.6	9.3	2.0	15.1	1.5
1960	23.8	9.5	1.9	16.3	1.6
1957	25.2	9.5	1.6	17.2	1.7
1955	24.9	9.3	2.0	17.6	1.8
1952	25.0	9.6	1.5	16.9	1.7
1950	23.9	9.6	2.0	16.3	1.6
1947	26.5	10.1	1.6	18.3	1.8
1945	20.5	11.0	1.2	10.4	1.0
1942	22.2	10.4	0.6	12.7	1.3
1940	19.4	10.8	0.6	9.2	0.9
1937	18.7	11.3	0.4	7.9	0.8
1935	18.7	10.9	0.3	8.0	0.8

NOTES: [a]Rates are expressed per thousand population, except percent figures. [b]Refers to net civilian immigration.

SOURCE: Adapted from Department of Commerce, Bureau of the Census, *Current Population Reports*, Series p–25, No. 418, 1969.

immigration remains relatively constant. In 1968 immigration accounted for over 22 percent of population growth compared with less than 10 percent in 1957 when birth rates were high.

Changes in the social structure as a result of population growth are shown in the development of new and the expansion of old cities. Changes in transportation, migration patterns, and medical advances have altered social life from an agrarian and self-sustaining to a crowded, interdependent, and urban one. Life expectancy has increased to over seventy years. The family structure and related institutions have also changed. The number of children per family has decreased; apartment living, smog, traffic snarls, strikes, noise, and crime have increased. The nature of work has changed from manual labor and long hours with great privacy to skilled and semiskilled jobs with time clocks, assembly lines, and little privacy. Life styles in housing, clothing, and food have changed from rambling farms to cubicles, tenements, and row houses and from home-grown and handsewn to prepackaged merchandise. Political life now centers on urban politicians. State legislatures are still in the midst of change from rural to urban dominance, but national politicians have needed to woo the urban electorate for some time. Leisure time has increased, and the resulting social change is reflected in bowling leagues, television, travel, and educational expansion. There is great discontent in city life, which was once portrayed as utopian. Increased taxes to support recreation, education, public welfare, urban government, public utilities, airports, and the hundreds of other demands of increased population have led to a discontent which can be shown in elections, letters to newspapers, and migration to nonurban areas.

Francis Merrill notes several social and cultural factors which have contributed to the population increase in the United States.

1. *Land*: The land was rich, plentiful, and for generations practically free for the taking.
2. *Marriage*: The opportunity for land and economic independence encouraged early marriage.
3. *Family*: Children were an asset on the frontier and on the farm.
4. *Health*: Farm dwellers were relatively isolated and hence free from many of the infectious and contagious diseases found in the city.
5. *Food*: Famine was never a problem in a country with such rich natural resources.
6. *Religion*: In the early years, the Protestant faith strongly encouraged large families, an attitude heartily seconded by the Roman Catholic faith of later immigrants.
7. *Philosophy*: The philosophic outlook and general social attitudes of the American people were optimistic, a factor that led to high fertility.
8. *Immigration*: More than 30 million immigrants, most of them young adults in the most reproductive years, have come to this country since its founding.
9. *Contraception*: Contraceptive information was not widely dis-

seminated until recently, and artificial checks on conception have been lacking.

10. *Residence*: Throughout the nineteenth and early part of the twentieth centuries, the bulk of the population was rural and followed the tendency toward large families that accompanies this way of life.[2]

Statistics on population growth can show more than size increases. Populations are composed of segments which, when viewed separately, provide an analysis of the internal dynamics of population trends. Components which are important to education in America include age, sex, race, and geographical distribution.

Population Distribution by Age

America has been changing from a young society to a middle-age society since 1800. Population data show a shift in the age distribution from a median age of sixteen years in 1800 to a median age of about twenty-eight by the mid-1960s. In the nineteenth century there was a sizable proportion of children to adults and a small percentage of persons over sixty. These proportions have changed considerably. In 1850 about 50 percent of the population was under twenty, compared with 35 percent in 1940 and about 38 percent in 1968. The proportion of the population over 65 was about 2.5 percent in 1850, 6.8 percent in 1940, and 9.3 percent in 1962.[3] The 1968 data show that approximately 10 percent of the population is over 65.

Median age data are affected by fertility and mortality rates. High fertility and high mortality rates account for the low median age of the early 19th century. As fertility declined during the later 19th and early 20th centuries, the average age of the population increased. The baby boom following World War II and the stabilized mortality rates caused the median age to drop from the 1952 peak of 30 to the present average of about 28. The moderately declining birth rates (Table 5) of the 1960s indicate that the median age of the population will probably remain in a range of 25 to 30 for some time to come.

When the age distribution of population is divided into five year segments as shown in Figure I, the largest single group of people in 1968 was in the age bracket of five to nine years old. The age group zero to four declined in population between 1960 and 1968, while virtually all other five year age groups increased in size. The result of this change in population is that now for the first time in American history the number of persons aged sixty-five and over exceeds the number who are under age five. Schools over the past two decades have been expanding rapidly to account for dramatic increases in young student enrollments. A changing population requires changing educational considerations.

The aging population poses some social, economic, and educational considerations. Social considerations include the needs for increased old-age security, medical care, leisure-time activities, and concern over social alienation of the old. Economic considerations stem from the need to finance care for the elderly and from the general lack of economic productivity of persons over sixty-five. Educational interest in the older population is in areas of the educational leisure-time activities; preparing people to work with the aged in social work, nursing, and related employment; and the possible utilization of older people in educational establishments. A law school in San Francisco built its fine reputation by hiring only professors who had retired from other law schools.

Havighurst and Neugarten note another educational aspect of the increased median age of society. They suggest that there are now larger proportions of adults who can perform the work of the society. This (along with increased technology) reduces the need for children to work and permits children to spend more time in education.[4] Table 6 shows the rise in median age of the population.

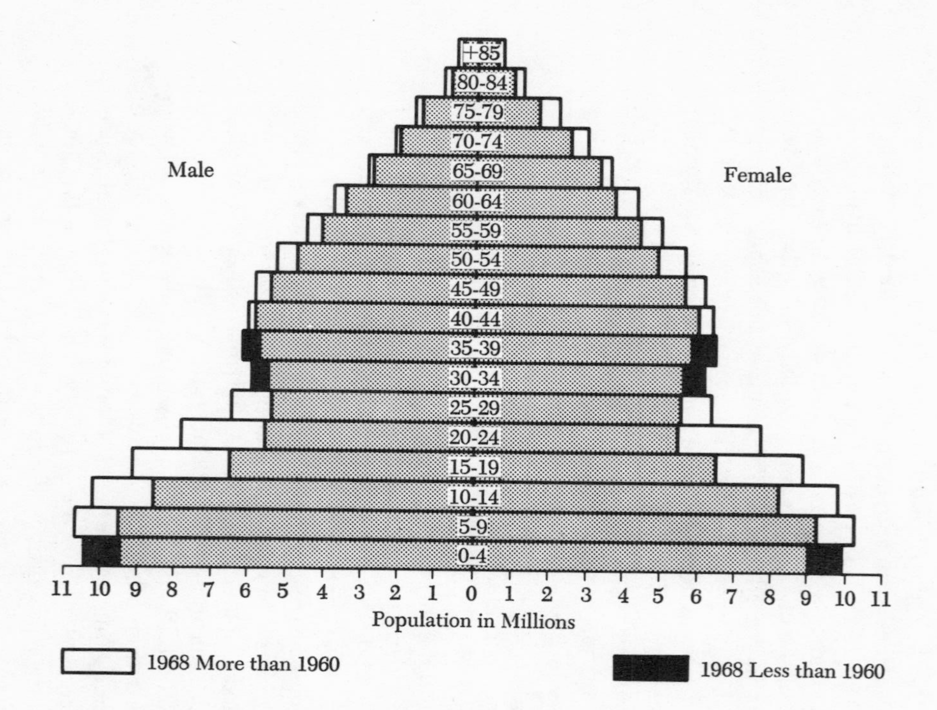

Figure 1. Population of the United States, by age and sex: 1968 and 1960. Note: Total population including Armed Forces overseas. (U.S. Department of Commerce, Bureau of the Census, *Current Population Reports*, Series p–25, No. 416, April 28, 1969.)

TABLE 6

Population by Race, Residence and Median Age, 1790–1968

Year	RACE[a]			RESIDENCE[b]		MEDIAN AGE		
	White	Black	Other	Urban	Rural	Total	White	Nonwhite
1968	176.6	22.3	2.2	127.5	70.8	27.7	28.6	21.5
1967	175.0	21.9	2.1	126.6	69.5	27.7	28.7	21.4
1966	173.3	21.6	2.0	125.2	68.9	27.8	28.7	21.4
1965	171.3	21.2	1.9	123.8	68.4	28.0	28.9	21.6
1960	158.8	18.8	1.6	125.2	54.0	29.4	30.2	23.4
1950	134.9	15.0	0.71	96.4	54.2	30.2	30.7	26.0
1940	118.2	12.8	0.58	74.4	57.2	29.0	29.5	25.2
1930	110.3	11.9	0.59	68.9	53.8	26.5	26.9	23.5
1920	94.8	10.4	0.42	54.1	51.5	25.3	25.6	22.4
1910	81.7	9.8	0.41	41.9	49.9	24.1	24.5	21.1
1900	66.8	8.8	0.35	30.1	45.8	22.9	23.4	19.7
1880	43.4	6.6	0.17	14.1	36.0	20.9	21.4	18.0
1860	26.9	4.4	0.07	6.2	25.2	19.4	19.7	17.5
1840	14.2	2.9	NA	1.8	15.2	17.8	17.9	17.3
1820	7.9	1.7	NA	0.6	8.9	16.7	16.5	17.2
1800	4.3	1.0	NA	0.3	4.9	NA	16.0	NA
1790	3.2	0.7	NA	0.2	3.7	NA	NA	NA

NOTES: [a]Race and residence figures given in millions, median age given in years of age.
NA indicates no data available.
Data up to 1960 include only coterminous U.S.
[b]Residence data corrected for 1965–1968 to present metropolitan and nonmetropolitan populations. Previously, urban areas included those with population in excess of 2,500. The 1965–1968 data reflect the standard metropolitan statistical area designation of 50,000 population.

SOURCE: Adapted from Department of Commerce, Bureau of the Census, Fifteenth Census Reports, *Population*, Vol 2; Sixteenth Census Reports, *Population*, Vol. 2, Part 1, and Vol. 4, Part 1; *U.S. Census of Population: 1950*, Vol. 2, Part 1; *U.S. Census of Population: 1960*, Vol 1; *Current Population Reports*, Series P–25, No. 416, Feb. 17, 1969; and *Statistical Abstract of the United States*, 1969.

Population Distribution by Sex

Composition of the United States population by sex has shown some interesting changes since 1820. Males consistently outnumbered females from 1820 to 1950, but in the past two decades females have outnumbered males. The ratio of men to women in 1900 was about 104 men to 100 women. In 1969 it had changed to 97 men per 100 women. Merrill suggests that the causes for this shift in sex distribution were:

1. The decline in immigration, which in its heaviest period during the early part of the present century was preponderantly male
2. The higher mortality rates for men than for women
3. The increase in the size of the peacetime Armed Forces during the decade of the 1950s.[5]

Male births outnumber female births, and the age-group data in Figure 1 illustrate that under age thirty males tend to outnumber females. From age thirty upward, however, females are the larger proportion of population.

Social and educational implications of this change in sex distribution in the population include a possible alteration in marriage and family arrangements, with larger numbers of unmarried women; changes in work patterns, utilizing more women in employment; and needs for increased educational opportunities for women.

Population Distribution by Race

Despite sizable Indian, Mexican, Puerto Rican, Chinese, and Japanese minorities, the preponderant nonwhite population in America is Negro or "black." For this reason we shall center our attention on the black and white groups. This of course, does not discount the social and educational impact of any ethnic group on the society, but instead concentrates on the largest segments. Certainly, for example, the educational problems posed by the social conditions of American Indians, Puerto Ricans, and other minority groups in America are worthy of full consideration. But the predominance of the white and black groups and the relevance for any other minority group of any educational and social change for the black population tends to overshadow specific problems of the other groups. This is unfortunate in the sense that social and educational injustice toward Mexicans and Chinese needs remedy also; nevertheless the prevalent movement in America toward increased civil rights, spearheaded by the black population, should have a transfer effect on the plight of others. The discussion of the white and black groups which follows has definite bearing on the problems posed by other minority distributions of population.

As Table 6 indicates, the relation of white to black population has changed in different ways over time. In 1800 approximately 23 percent of the population was black. By 1850, the proportion had dropped to less than 20 percent. In 1900, there were about 13 black citizens for each 100 white citizens. In the twentieth century blacks have maintained a population of about 10 to 12 percent of the white population. Between 1800 and 1950, the proportion of blacks to whites decreased, although both groups increased in size. Since the Civil War immigration of black men has dwindled greatly, while immigration of white men has remained relatively high. Since 1950, however, the rate of increase in population of nonwhites (including Negroes) has been much higher than the rate of increase of whites. Nonwhites increased at the rate of about 42 percent, while whites increased about 26 percent.[6]

The nonwhite population is very young in contrast to the white population. In 1968 the median age of nonwhites was 21.5 years of age while the median for whites was 28.6. This reflects differences in birth rates for whites and nonwhites over a period of time. Projections of population changes between now and 1985 anticipate a continuance in the median age differences between whites and nonwhites as well as continuance of higher birth rates for nonwhites than whites. The present projection for median ages of the population in 1985 is nineteen to twenty-five years of age for nonwhites, twenty-seven to thirty years of age for whites.[7]

Anyone who reads current newspapers is aware of the general dimensions of the educational problems resulting from minority-group populations. The melting pot myth that America melts all ethnic groups into a happy oneness has been exploded in recent studies.[8] The assimilation process, in which education plays a major role, is more difficult and complex than has been thought. This is especially true when assimilation involves racism. The evolution of racism from slavery and socially contrived inferiority causes extreme problems in assimilation and socialization. The inequality of social opportunity and condition which has befallen the blacks and other minorities is continued in the educational system. Educational opportunities, aspirations, facilities, and achievements are lower for members of the black population, who are victims of the disparity in social norms. Table 7 compares these educational differences between blacks and whites. Nonwhite educational attainments since 1950 are compared to white attainments in Figure 2.

As Figure 2 shows, black students are completing high school in dramatically higher percentages since 1950, but have made only slight increases in the proportions of students completing college. This may change in the near future as a result of student revolts and groups like the Black Student Union and Afro-American student organizations which have been active in changing restrictive admissions policies on college campuses. When colleges with the prestige of Harvard, Yale, Princeton, and Dartmouth significantly increase enrollments of black students, as was the case in the 1969–1970 academic year, other higher education institutions also increase these opportunities. Many other institutions had much higher proportional enrollments of black students than the Ivy League schools, but had less national status. The current trend to expanded admissions for minority group students at major state universities like

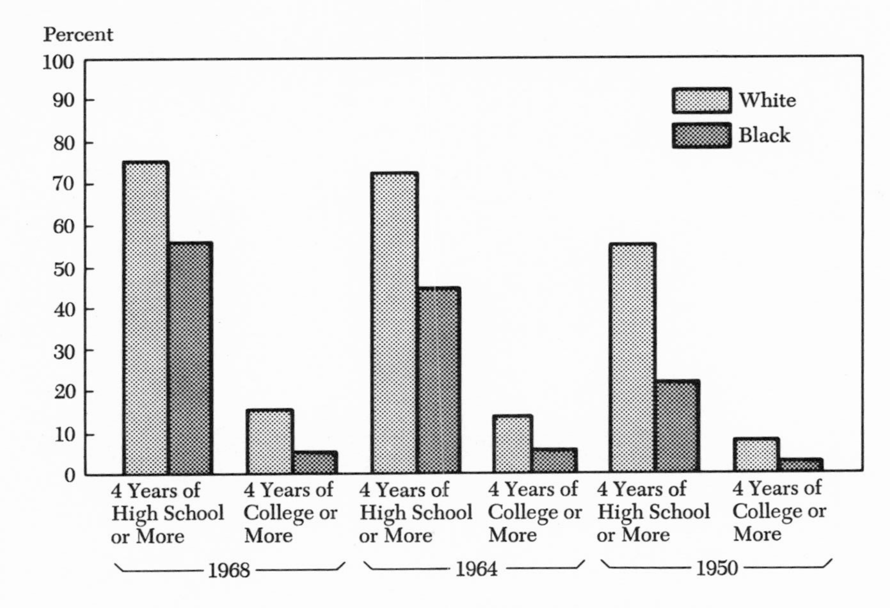

Figure 2. Percent of population age 25 to 29 who completed 4 years of high school or more or 4 years of college or more, by race, for the United States: 1968, 1964, and 1950. (U.S. Department of Commerce, Bureau of the Census, *Current Population Reports*, Series p–20, No. 182, April 28, 1969.)

TABLE 7

Black and White Students Enrolled in Grades 1 and 12, by Area and by Racial Composition of Schools: 1965

	RACIAL COMPOSITION OF SCHOOLS							
	0 to 10% Black		10 to 20% Black		20 to 80% Black		80 to 100% Black	
Grade, Area, and Region	Black	White	Black	White	Black	White	Black	White
All regions, grade 1	3.8	79.9	2.4	9.6	21.8	9.8	72.0	0.7
Metropolitan:								
North and West	3.8	79.7	4.5	9.1	47.2	9.0	44.5	1.3
South and Southwest	2.2	89.7	0.5	0.9	2.0	9.2	95.3	0.2
Nonmetropolitan:								
North and West	19.6	80.1	7.0	11.3	45.0	8.5	28.4	0.1
South and Southwest	4.2	70.9	2.1	16.6	15.9	12.1	77.8	0.4
All regions, grade 12	10.0	79.9	5.1	9.6	23.2	10.3	61.7	0.2
Metropolitan:								
North and West	13.0	72.2	8.3	8.2	54.8	17.4	23.9	0.2
South and Southwest	2.9	92.3	1.2	5.9	1.2	1.6	94.7	0.2
Nonmetropolitan:								
North and West	51.7	88.6	16.8	7.3	23.7	4.1	7.8	[a]
South and Southwest	7.7	71.5	3.6	20.2	5.5	8.2	83.2	0.1

NOTE: [a]Less than 0.05 percent.

Michigan, Rutgers, California and others should alter the data shown in Figure 2.

The racial composition of schools and corresponding geographical regions are shown in Table 7. Although only first and twelfth grades are shown, the data indicate the racial imbalance of schools. In metropolitan regions of the North and West about 80 percent of white students attend schools which have less than 10 percent black enrollment while 44.5 percent of black students attend schools composed of over 80 percent black enrollment. The data show that the imbalance is even more pronounced in Southern and Southwestern metropolitan areas. In these, almost 90 percent of the white students attend schools with 10 percent or less black enrollments, while over 95 percent of the black students attend schools of virtually all-black population. Nonmetropolitan schools are somewhat more balanced in both areas. These data are for 1965, despite the 1954 Supreme Court ruling requiring desegregation of schools.

An increase in educational attainment, however, does not guarantee a corresponding increase in occupation or income. As Figure 3 illustrates, black employed males had lower levels of education than did whites in general, but where the level of education was equivalent, blacks had fewer white-collar jobs and less income. Even where the type of job and level of education were equivalent, black men received less income than white men.

Because of the impact of recent developments in politics and education, it is important to note that segregation–integration data may be affected. In the political realm, the government's decision to use courts rather than fund cut-offs to pursue integration had not been fully tested at the time of this writing. Some argue that long delays will result and integration will decline; especially in the South. Others maintain that integration will be more rapid.

A second development is the increasing demand of blacks for local control of all-black schools. This segregation is proposed because integration has presumably not been effective, and some black leaders prefer to improve black schools rather

Employed Black men had less education than employed white men.

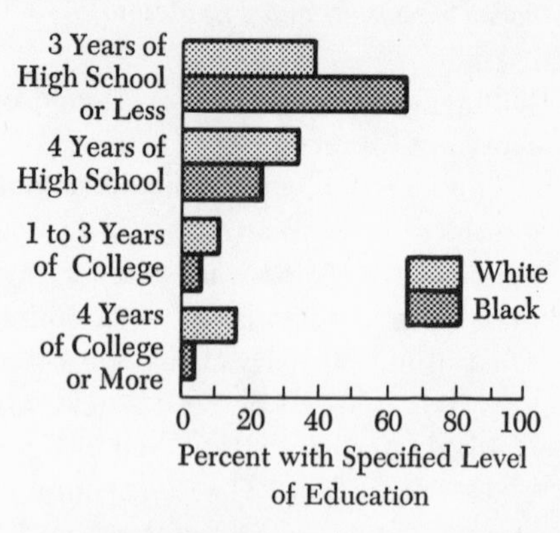

Among workers with a given amount of education, Black men were less likely to hold a white-collar job than were white men.

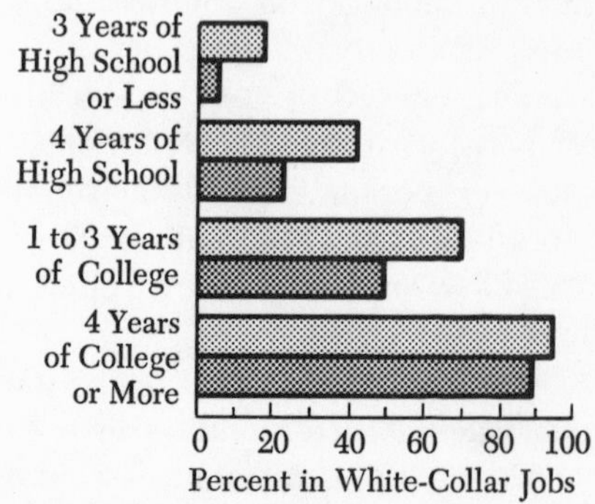

Among workers with a given type of job and a given amount of education, Black men had less income than their white counterparts.

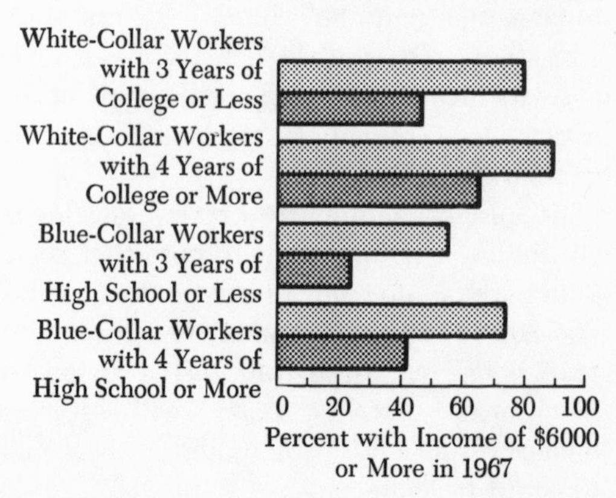

Figure 3. Education attainment, occupation, and income of employed white and black males, 25 to 64 years old: March 1968. (U.S. Department of Commerce, Bureau of the Census, *Current Population Reports*, Series p–20, No. 182, April 28, 1969.)

than support integration at this time. This can alter integration data.

A third development may affect integration in a substantial way. It has already become a provocative argument in the intellectual community and has been used to support opposition to integration by some local communities. Arthur Jensen rocked the educational world when he presented data linking scores on intelligence tests to race.[9] This argument, a renewal of the heredity–environment battles of early social sciences, was rekindled by the publication of Jensen's work. The implication drawn from his analysis of the link between race and intelligence is that blacks are innately inferior in those characteristics measured by IQ tests. A flurry of writing opposing Jensen's position developed quickly.[10] The contrary arguments contended that IQ tests are culturally loaded to white language and customs and do not adequately test intelligence; that IQ scores are more closely associated with social class than race; and that unequal opportunities for blacks in the society for centuries account for the differences in IQ scores and are environmental, not hereditary. This argument is not likely to subside easily. Both positions have large quantities of data and differing interpretations.

There is agreement, however, between Jensen and his critics that regardless of the basis for differences in IQ scores, there is no rationale for inferior educational treatment of any segment of the society. Yet, the schools have a long history of neglect for minority group students. The education of American Indians exemplifies this maltreatment. The Bureau of Indian Affairs was founded with the explicit aim to alienate Indian children "from their native culture and language so they could take their place in modern society."[11] After a century of this questionable service to Indians we find in 1969 that 90 percent of the Indians in the U.S. live in substandard housing, including 50,000 in dilapidated structures that cannot be classified as houses; 40 percent of the Indians are unemployed; the life span for Indians is about forty-three years compared with sixty-five to seventy years for whites; death from tuberculosis is seven times that of whites; and American Indians have the highest suicide rate of any ethnic group in the world.[12] These data are indirect results of the education of American Indians.

About 55,000 Indian children are in government schools, while approximately 16,000 are not enrolled in any school.[13] Indian community involvement in schools is virtually non-existent. Literacy rates of Indians are among the lowest in the country. Ten percent of American Indians have had no formal education while 60 percent have less than an eighth grade education.[14] These data are symptomatic of the dimensions of unequal education. Similar race or social class inequalities are evident in educational provisions for Mexican-Americans, migrant farm workers and urban poor.

Geographical Population Distribution

Social mobility can be both vertical and horizontal. *Vertical mobility* refers to movement by social class and is discussed in Chapter 9. *Horizontal mobility* refers to changes in the distribution of population as a result of internal migration: the movement of large numbers of people from one part of the country to another. Both the continuing westward shift of population and the population movement from rural to urban areas constitute illustrations of horizontal mobility.

Where are the jobs?

The urbanization process, which has had such dramatic effects on the nature of American life, began in the mid-1800s. As can be calculated from Table 6, about 7 percent of the population lived in urban areas in 1850. This figure had changed to about 40 percent by 1900 and about 70 percent by 1960. Furthermore, of the rural population remaining in 1960, those living on farms constituted less than half.

Urbanization is important to sociologists because cities have tended to dominate the culture. Social relations and interactions differ according to the nature of population-migration patterns; social behaviors, statuses, and roles vary according to the social environment in which they occur; and social institutions such as government, family, religion, recreation, and education are all susceptible to change according to environment. The change in population from small, relatively isolated farms and villages to urban centers is a particularly noteworthy social phenomenon.

Two other population distribution processes have become increasingly important to sociology and education in recent times: *metropolitanization,* the development of sprawling intermingling urban and suburban areas, and *suburbanization,* the migration of people from urban and rural areas into politically distinct suburban areas. These two processes are now at work in American society. Sometimes they operate harmoniously through a metropolitan, coordinated plan of joint development of urban and suburban areas, and sometimes they operate discordantly, resulting in urban-suburban hostilities, separation, and discontent. In most metropolitan areas both harmony and discord exist. Public utilities and highways shared by urban and suburban people may result in positive relations, while police, fire, and school systems politically and economically separate, may lead to social frictions because of disparate expenses, salaries, and services. Eventually, due to economic pressures and the realization of interdependence, suburban areas may be encompassed by metropolitan government, but at present metropolitanization suffers from the handicap of being antithetical to the motivations for suburban living.

At one time the lure to suburbs was based on a romantic, back-to-nature myth that caused city dwellers to leave the evils of crowded, smoggy cities for the fresh, open areas of the suburbs. More recently, the flight to the suburbs also has involved the attempt of middle-class whites to leave the burgeoning black ghettoes that many cities are becoming. If the rate of urban-suburban migration by race continues as it has during this past decade, the major cities of the country will be populated mainly by black people.

As a corollary to the suburban attractions of open space and escape from integration, the improvement of transportation, technology, shopping areas, and development of suburban economic power have contributed to speed the rate of population increase in the suburbs. Between 1950 and 1960 the population grew by about 28 million. About 85 percent of this increase occurred in just 212 metropolitan areas. And, while the central city area grew about 9 percent, the suburban surrounding areas grew about 17 percent.

Education has reflected this mobility in many ways. While the city was a thriving society, the city schools enjoyed the prestige of higher expenses per child in school, larger salaries for teachers, better collections of books, and more comprehensive facilities and equipment than suburban schools. As the strong middle-class support of public schools shifted to suburban areas, urban schools have been financially crippled and culturally starved. They are the subject of a vast amount of research, rhetoric, restructuring, and evaluation. In many respects the urban school is passing through a social-consciousness phase reminiscent of the concerns over rural education several decades ago. At that time society became very aware of problems in rural schools, and various agencies—Federal, state and local—developed structures for examining and improving rural schools. A similar development is now in evidence in regard to urban schools.

Summary

The era of mass man has been influential in altering social structure, social problems, and social institutions. While this can be demonstrated in a variety of ways, the data on population dynamics provides a factual background to the situation. This chapter proposed ways in which changes in population affect institutions as well as individuals, and presented a selection of the massive amounts of demographic information available in contemporary America. Since the school is a major social institution, it is imperative that analyses of the school perceive it in its social context. One aspect of this context is demography.

NOTES

1. See Kingsley Davis, "Population," *Scientific American*, vol. 209, pp. 63–71, September, 1963; J.O. Hertzler, *The Crisis in World Population*, University of Nebraska Press, Lincoln, Nebr., 1956; Philip M. Hauser, "World Population Trends," *Sociology and Social Research*, vol. 39, pp. 73–80, November, 1954; Carl Sax, *Standing Room Only*, Beacon Press, Boston, 1955.
2. Francis E. Merrill, *Society and Culture: An Introduction to Sociology*, Prentice-Hall, Englewood Cliffs, N.J., 1965, pp. 226–227.
3. Robert J. Havighurst and Bernice L. Neugarten, *Society and Education*, Allyn and Bacon, Boston, 1967, pp. 301–302; Merrill, pp. 235–236.
4. Havighurst & Neugarten, pp. 301–302.
5. Merrill, pp. 236–237.
6. *Ibid.*, pp. 238–239.
7. Department of Commerce, Bureau of the Census, *Current Population Reports*, "Population Estimates," Series P–25, No. 416, Feb. 17, 1969, p. 10.
8. Nathan Glazer and Daniel P. Moynihan, *Beyond the Melting Pot: The Negroes, Puerto Ricans, Jews, Italians, and Irish of New York City*, M.I.T. and Harvard University Presses, Cambridge, Mass.; reviewed by D. W. Brogan, "New York's Unmelted Pot," *Encounter*, vol. 22, no. 6, June, 1964, pp. 55–60.
9. Arthur Jensen, "Social Class, Race, and Genetics: Implications for Education," *American Educational Research Journal*, January, 1968 pp. 1–42; Martin Deutsch, Irwin Katz, and Arthur Jensen, *Social Class, Race and Psychosocial Development*, Holt, Rinehart and Winston, New York, 1968; Arthur Jensen, "How Much Can We Boost IQ and Scholastic Achievement?" *Harvard Educational Review*, Winter, 1969, pp. 1–123.
10. Harvard Educational Review, *Environment, Heredity and Intelligence*, Harvard University Press, Cambridge, 1969; Jerome Kagan, J. McV. Hunt, *et. al.*, "How Much Can We Boost IQ and Scholastic Achievement? A Discussion," *Harvard Educational Review*, Spring, 1969, pp. 274–356.
11. Peter Farb, "The American Indian: A Portrait in Limbo," *Saturday Review*, October 12, 1968, p. 27.
12. Lyndon Baines Johnson, "The Forgotten American," Presidential Message to Congress, March 6, 1968, *Weekly Compilation of Presidential Documents*, U.S. Government Printing Office, Vol. 4, 1968.
13. D. Henninger and N. Esposito, "Indian Schools," *New Republic*, February 15, 1969, pp. 18–21.
14. Johnson, "Forgotten American," *op. cit.*

Chapter 9 / *Social Class, Caste, and Mobility*

Social stratification refers to the structural relationship of social hierarchies which conveys more cultural privileges to one group of people than to another. It is the result of a cultural tradition which permits members to perform differing roles with differing social rewards. Evolution of social ranking by birth, position, wealth, prowess, or other criteria occurs within each society and is based upon the particular mores of that society. Thus, in a primitive hunting society the best hunters may be given the greatest social privilege. In an industrialized society, social recognition may go to wealth measured in industrial terms. In monarchial society, social status is granted solely on hereditary grounds. The separation and ranking of groups having similar social status within a society are two means of identifying social stratification. Societies can be seen in terms of social power, as vertical stratifications, with groups with the least power at the bottom, and those with the most power at the top.

Two forms of social stratification are caste and class. A *caste* is a specifically defined, rigidly controlled group whose membership is usually based on heredity. A person is born into a caste, high or low, and he remains in it regardless of his abilities or achievements. A caste system does not permit upward social mobility from one caste to another, and typically does not permit intermarriage between members of differing castes. A *class* is a group of people who have similar social status in a hierarchy of classes. It is a category, less rigidly defined than caste, in which membership depends upon wealth, prestige, social behaviors, hereditary position, and related factors. A child is a member of a class at birth, but a class system permits some social mobility based on abilities, achievements, and sometimes pure ambition. Thus a class system is more fluid than a caste system. When a class system tightens the boundaries between classes and imposes rigid requirements for mobility, it becomes more like a caste system.

The social class system in the United States bears some resemblance to a caste system. Hereditary wealth and social position are still strong determinants of later social status. The status of a child of upper-class origin presumably will not be altered despite his lack of ability or achievement. At the extremes of social class in the United States a change in social status is most difficult. Mobility occurs most readily among classes between these extremes.

Determinants of Social Class

There are several measures of social class in America. Hodgkinson[1] identifies the following four systems of analyzing social classes.

1. *Discrete, closed classes.* Appearing mainly in studies of communities in the 1930s and 1940s, this approach to social-class analysis utilized anthropological methods of research. W. Lloyd Warner was a particularly prolific and provocative researcher of this approach; his thesis was that a six-class system of social stratification was typical of the American community.

The six classes were upper-upper (about 1.4 percent of the population), lower-upper (about 1.6 percent), upper-middle (10 percent), lower-middle (28 percent), upper-lower (33 percent), and lower-lower (25 percent). Thus, the main classes—upper, middle, and lower—formed a three-step pyramid with the lower class constituting approximately 58 percent, the middle class 38 percent, the upper class 3 percent of the population. Hodgkinson contends that Warner's position of six stable, rather discrete social classes was based on studies of small, relatively closed communities and would not be supportable in the more fluid, urban society of today.[2]

2. *The Social Class as a Continuum*. This viewpoint posits that social classes cannot be categorized into separate entities. It presumes that no fixed classes exist, and that there is considerable overlapping between perceived social statuses. This overlapping is as important as the classes themselves and establishes a link from the uppermost to the lowermost groups in a society. This approach, assuming society's interrelationship with demarcation points used only as reference data, suffers from a lack of empirical justification because it tends to destroy a classification system and the numerical measures that classification permits. It is easy to explain the multiclass values and friendships that permeate this society with this analysis, but it becomes difficult to make any meaningful differentiations among classes.

3. *Individual Consciousness of Class*. Hodgkinson cites a study by Richard Centers on *The Psychology of Social Classes*[3] to support this means of analyzing social class. Centers' analysis relies heavily on the perceptions of persons as to their own ranking in a class hierarchy; that is, how individuals place themselves in a class structure. The blue-collar worker and the white-collar worker tend to be aware of differences between their groups, but within these broad occupational groups there is very limited further distinction.

4. *Status Consistency and Class*. This approach is concerned with each person's status in relation to his fellow actors and the development of tests to judge how much the status ratings tend to remain consistent for the individual throughout his most

important activities. Consistent status rankings would be a measure of class. Comparisons of consistency are possible, and recent sociological research shows some promise in this approach. The four factors utilized in this analysis are occupation, income, education, and ethnic origin. Studies indicate that for some people status in each may be different. That is, there may be a consistency in status ranking by income that does not occur in occupation. Hodgkinson notes that a large amount of research needs to be done on the dimensions of status ranking and the developmental patterns of status. He raises the question of automobile ownership as one dimension of status, and suggests that more work be undertaken to investigate why high rankings of social status which children ascribe to particular occupations, like policeman or mailman, change as the children grow older. The developmental status-ranking problem is an interesting area for continuing research, especially with regard to education. What impact does education have on perceptions of high-status occupations and on status in general? Even within the formal system of education, what determines the relative status rankings of pupils, teachers, administrators, professors, boards of education, and parents?

Measures of Social Class

No matter what approach to the analysis of social class a sociologist follows, he must depend upon the development of criterion measures for judging class position. Most investigators have utilized quantifiable social aspects of living as criteria. W. Lloyd Warner and his associates developed a series of scales of two varieties. One included ratings by trained observers and incorporated such data as matching information on class placement from several interviewees; rating by the subject's reputation as inferior or superior; comparing the subject with others whose social class had already been established, and rating him by membership in clubs, organizations, churches, and so forth.

The second set of scales was the Index of Status Characteristics which used data about occupation, source of income, and type of dwelling, and dwelling area.[4]

Joseph Kahl outlined the main dimensions of class, and thus the areas for measurement, as follows:

1. *Prestige*, the level of respect
2. *Occupation*, based on level of income, social value, and necessary requirements for entrance
3. *Possessions*, including wealth and type and nature of income
4. *Social interaction*, who comes into contact with whom
5. *Class consciousness*, awareness of an individual's own status in relation to others
6. *Value orientations*, what is considered to be important or right
7. *Power*, control of, or by, others.[5]

A third generally accepted measure is illustrated in the Centers studies cited earlier. Centers defines social class ". . . as a psychological phenomenon in the fullest sense of the term. That is, a man's class is a part of his ego, a feeling on his part of belongingness to something; an identification with something larger than himself."[6] The class consciousness noted by Kahl, then, becomes a major measure of social class for Centers. The class into which a person places himself is a means of judging his social status, since the perception of class, according to Centers, is related to a person's subjective values, mores, and attitudes regarding his own position in the status hierarchy. Data from Centers' work showed that virtually all Americans were aware of social-class distinctions, although not in the terms which had been used earlier to separate upper from lower classes. Using a three-class breakdown—upper, middle, and working—Centers found that 3 percent of his sample responded that they were in the upper class; 34 percent indicated middle-class membership, and 51 percent described themselves as members of the working class. Only 1 percent acknowledged lower-class membership, and 1 percent stated that they did not believe in social classes.[7]

The important point here is not the technical aspect of measuring social class, but the realization that classes can be identified and values ascribed to their members, even though one class may overlap into another. Whether measured in relatively objective terms like source of income, occupation, and area of residence, or in subjective terms like class consciousness and attitudes, there are firm data to show that some differences among members of the society are linked to social status within that society. Although class distinctions may not be clear in each case, there do seem to be characteristics which separate classes.

Social Mobility

A social-class system, as opposed to the caste system, provides some opportunity for movement from one class to another. In the United States this mobility among classes operates mainly between the working class and the middle class. If the six-class schemata of upper-upper, lower-upper, upper-middle, lower-middle, upper-lower, and lower-lower classes is used, the mobility is more obvious since individuals can cross class boundary lines in a measurable way. The greatest mobility in this system occurs among the upper-lower, lower-middle, and upper-middle classes. Since the boundary lines between classes are arbitrary designations, it is perhaps more worthwhile to consider the means of social mobility in this society and their impact on the schools. A rigid definition of particular classes will be avoided, because of our skepticism that such definitions are meaningful. This creates some problems in discussing social mobility, but if one views social classes as somewhat fluid, then mobility can be seen as the dynamics of the fluid.

Individuals can move among and within social classes both upward and downward. This mobility depends upon the acquisition or loss of specific behaviors, accepted values, and socially approved symbols. Movement downward can occur in the middle group by socially unacceptable behavior like alcoholism, crime convictions, attempted suicide, drug addiction, or dropping out of school. If an attorney who has achieved the characteristics of an upper-middle-class member has a son who is not able to remain in college or who becomes an alcoholic or a criminal, the son will fall below social-class expectations and acquire a lower social status. Since one of the characteristics of an upwardly mobile family is great sensitivity to the behaviors of each of the family's members, the attorney's son becomes a family liability and is subject to ostracism and greater pressures to adopt the class mores of the family. This can, of course, result in even further alienation of the son from the family. Signs of downward mobility in their children cause great distress in families struggling to achieve upward mobility. Upper-class families may have sufficient status and power to cover the downward behaviors of offspring and to protect the family status by remaining socially aloof and by severely limiting the social participation of any members who exhibit downward tendencies. Families in the lowest social segment usually are not involved in attempts to improve their hierarchical standing, and thus have no significant stake in the social behaviors of their children. The extremes of social class, then, are much less mobile than the middle section, and this mobility puts great stress on class members to achieve in one form or another.

The American creed of success, which emphasizes upward mobility, almost fails to acknowledge the fact that many people lose social status during their lives. Wilensky and Edwards found that among the urban working class, about 20 percent suffered socially as "skidders." These people held positions lower in social status at the end of their lives than at the beginning.[8] Yet expectancies of upward mobility permeate American society, its status consciousness, its Horatio Alger literature and movies, and its measurable symbols of success. These expectancies create great anxieties and frustrations for those who participate in the social climb. It places particular stress on education in the society, a point which will be discussed later.

Just as alcoholism and drug addiction are means of downward mobility, marriage, athletic ability, occupational change, social intelligence, and education are means of upward mobility. While a caste system is endogamous, permitting marriage only within the caste, the class system permits interclass marriage. There are, however, some caste-like factors in American society in regard to marriage. The legal and social restrictions against miscegenation (marriage between races) are examples of the operation of a caste society in regard to marriage. Laws in some southern states have prohibited blacks from marrying whites, and social restrictions existing throughout the country carry the same prohibition. Within the white social system there is the opportunity to gain status by marriage. This is more typically true for females than males. A secretary marrying her executive boss gains status, as does a chorus girl marrying into a wealthy family.

In an era of great interest in athletic competition, the ability to perform in physical contests is another means for upward social mobility. This is especially true of boys from working-class backgrounds who develop sufficient athletic prowess to get scholarships to college or lucrative positions on professional teams.

Occupation also is closely associated with social class. Most investigators use occupation as one of the main criteria for determining social status. It would follow, then, that a change in occupation from unskilled to skilled, or from junior executive to executive, or from a lower social-value job to a higher one represents an upwardly mobile individual. The boy who takes a job as stock-room clerk and becomes department manager over a period of time has changed social status to some degree. If he successfully opens his own store, he increases his status further. If he quits as stock clerk to take a job in management training in a different field, his status is temporarily altered and his future status depends upon success in management.

Intelligence is a means for upward mobility, since intelligence, as it is now measured, has a cultural base. It usually refers to the level of ability for performing culturally determined activities. In the United States, intelligence is directly related to communication skills, including mathematical symbols. Among primitive tribes, whose survival depends on food gathering, intelligence must include skills of using the cultural tools and environment for hunting and fishing. Our measures of intelligence are closely linked to social success, and the individual who desires upward mobility must have sufficient facility with intelligence factors such as vocabulary and numerical skill. This has an obvious relation to education, because a primary function of the school is to provide these basic intellectual skills. This does not mean that intelligence and education are necessarily linked with regard to social mobility. Anderson suggests that intelligence is a greater factor than education in upward mobility.[9] He studied mobility data from the United States, England, and Sweden and found that differences in intelligence were more related to upward mobility than education alone, although education was one of many factors influencing upward mobility.[10] The generally accepted position is that education is a particularly important means of social mobility in American society.

Education, Social Class, and Mobility

Whether one views social class as a system of distinct units separated by arbitrary lines into five or six categories or as a continuum of social statuses which are relatively fluid, disparities in social position do exist in American society. Some groups have more social and economic power than others and can exert more social control. Education appears to be associated with the disparities in status and with the changes in status referred to as mobility. Warner,[11] Hollingshead,[12] and Havighurst[13] have studied the relation of social class to education, and, as Havighurst reports in a summary of studies, "The kind of education an American child gets depends very much on the social-class position of his family."[14] Havighurst's analysis of a Midwestern city in 1958 showed that children of the lower classes dropped out of school at rates from 5 to 30 times as high as children from middle-class families, while children from the middle and upper-lower classes entered college in a proportion 16 to 22 times as high as lower-lower-class children.[15] He noted that the trend in college entrance for working-class children has been substantially upward since the 1920s. By 1960 the number of college students from working-class families was greater than the number from upper- and upper-middle-class families.[16] This is the result of a number of factors:

1. There is a cultural agreement on the value of education which seems to transcend social-class boundaries. The only exceptions are in the minute extremes of class where education apparently has limited value. The middle-class value attached to education is greater than that found in the class extremes, but the generalization that education is a "good" activity has wide acceptability in American society.

2. Since education, even without regard to its function in social mobility, is considered a worthy endeavor of all citizens, there has been a continuing move to provide more mass education. This has stimulated public investment in colleges offering inexpensive and easily accessible higher education. This current development in higher education is strikingly similar to earlier developments in American secondary education.

3. The obvious use of education to improve social status is a third factor that has caused working-class children to seek college entrance. A common belief about education is that more education brings better jobs, better jobs bring better income, and all three bring higher social status. This cultural belief in education, which differs from the idea that education is of value in itself, sees the schools as tools of social leverage, and the accumulation of education as one measure of class standing. There has been considerable support given to free, public education in America by the labor movement and others who perceive education as a means of social mobility. Families have taken the general position that children should be better off than their parents—and that this includes being better educated.

Class attitudes toward education affect the social expectations of schools. A suburban or urban school which serves mainly upwardly mobile middle-class families is under intense pressure to provide the proper education to get children into colleges, and often even into the higher ranking colleges. This pressure causes schools and teachers to install highly academic requirements for virtually all children in the institution, regardless of abilities or interests. Concomitant pressure exists in the home, where success in schoolwork is viewed as a major prognosis of success in life. The teacher who does not assign homework in large quantities or fails to threaten students adequately with low marks is seen as a heretic by the system. In a similar way, urban and suburban schools which tend to have students from working-class families often lock them into specialized vocational or technical programs which prepare them only for positions related to their social-class origins.

American education tends to be reflective of middle-class values, attitudes, and symbols. The schools should, according to this ethic, prepare good, solid citizens; armed with speaking and calculating proficiency; clean of mind, thought, and deed; and concerned with getting a good job. Students are expected to be pleasant, relatively docile, to speak when spoken to and to give specific answers, to do neat work, not to cause trouble, to be respectful, not to ask embarrassing questions, to be stylish in appearance, to have money, to participate in school affairs; in short, to conform.

Schools tend to expect students to cheat, and the in-and-out-of-school pressures to succeed ensure the occurrence of cheating. Elaborate procedures often are developed in schools to prohibit or limit it, it is socially unacceptable, and school punishments exist to maintain the values of a middle-class society; nevertheless the social emphasis on educational success creates a strong temptation for cheating. Students are not expected to challenge teachers, the school system, or the society. Controversial issues are normally outside the scope of activity of the school because the issues may cause students to question the values they are being socialized to adopt. Middle-class success symbols like new clothing, pocket money, a car in high school, and dates at appropriate places are observable in the school culture.

Social class has other impacts upon the schools. The relation of class to social pathology among youngsters who are intimidated, shy, or fearful, as well as ones who are aggressive, is notable. Havighurst has pointed out that most of this pathology among children occurs in the lower working class—the lowest 20 percent on a social class scale.[17] His rationale for this aggressiveness or withdrawal, which bothers many schools and teachers, is that the children are deprived in their environments. He notes three forms of deprivation which seem to effect these children most: (1) *affectional*: inadequate affection, (2) *model*: lack of socially acceptable people as models for imitation, and (3) *intellectual*: insufficient stimulus for affairs of the mind. Havighurst notes that these deprivations are by no means characteristic of all, or even a majority, of those who fall into the low 20 percent.[18] What he is arguing is that the largest proportion of this behavioral pathology among children occurs among this level of social class. It is obvious that a school which has middle-class values and expects middle-class behavior experiences difficulties in dealing with excessive withdrawal or aggressiveness. Deviant behavior is treated in other sections of this book, but the social-class background which conditions behavioral expectations and those who deviate from them should not be overlooked.

Another area of class concern is that of decision making. The potent forces in American education tend to come from the upper-middle segment of the society. Warner analyzed the Board of Education in "Jonesville." He found that, in practice, members of the board came from the upper two classes, were always men, and never were Catholics, Jews, Irishmen, or Democrats, despite the theoretical opportunity for any adult person to be elected.[19] The Rotarians, according to Warner, were proud of the manner by which they had controlled the selection of board members.[20] He also writes that no board member was found who believed that the community should provide high school education for all adolescents. His interviews with board members showed that they thought that many boys and girls are better off not going to school, that, generally, only those of the top three social classes benefit from high school. They felt that children of the upper-lower class benefited if they adopted middle-class behaviors and that children of the lower-lower class hadn't enough ability to benefit from high school.[21] Although Warner's study is over two decades old, it is still relatively accurate in its portrayal of school boards.

Membership on boards is controlled in most areas by social class and ethnic considerations. W. W. Charters analyzed 62 studies of school-board composition and found that virtually all reported that board members were selected from the upper-middle class. He indicates that the member's social-class position does not seem to influence his vote on educational matters.[22] There is a tacit agreement in some strongly Catholic areas of the Northeast to allocate elected school-board seats to Catholic representatives. In other areas the dominant national group—Italian, Swedish, Irish, or Polish—maintains control of board membership. In most cases, even including ethnic considerations, boards are composed of members of the higher social classes. This has been one of the more frustrating problems of the black ghettos, where education is beginning to mean mobility; but the black community, in and out of the ghetto, has severely limited access to Board of Education membership and decision making. In recent times there have been increasing numbers of board members from labor, and a few from the black community, but the general statement of relation between higher social classes and school-board membership remains relatively accurate.[23] A 1965 Report of the National School Boards Association shows board membership to be comprised 35 percent of businessmen, 27 percent of professional and technical persons, 12 percent of farmers, 7 percent of housewives, and 6 percent of clerks and skilled workers.[24]

Other determinants of decision making in schools—the administrators, prominent parent groups, other school pressure groups, and teachers—are affected by social class and mobility dimensions. Teachers and administrators are either upwardly mobile or have adopted middle-class values; vocal parent groups tend to reflect class biases toward college entrance, curriculum, homework, and so forth; and other pressure groups like community service clubs, bank and business operators, and patriotic associations which seek conformity of behavior, present a social-class ethic to the schools which does not condone deviant class behaviors or values.

A review of research related to the sociology of education by William M. Cave and Donald L. Halsted notes the importance of social-class factors to education.[25] Cave and Halsted include studies by Edward McDill and James Coleman which suggest that peer status within the institution may be of greater influence on interest in higher education and achievement than social-class origins.[26] Nevertheless, they state that "the saliency of the social-class variable has been noted in numerous studies predicting such phenomena as student achievement, expectations, aspirations, and behavior."[27]

T. H. Marshall, in a series of lectures presented at Cambridge University, described the use of education as a "class-making" and "class-abating" device. In referring to an earlier English school system, which offered free public elementary education for children of families that could not afford the private schools, Marshall states:

> The old elementary schools, though open to all, were used by a social class (admittedly a very large and varied one) for which no other kind of education was available. Its numbers were brought up in segregation from the higher classes and under influences which set their stamp on the children subjected to them. "Ex-elementary school-boy" became a label which a man might carry through life, and it pointed to a distinction which was real, and not merely conventional, in character. For a divided educational system, by promoting both intra-class similarity and inter-class difference, gave emphasis and precision to a criterion of social distance.[28]

Marshall goes on to note that the development of a secondary education system open to all has altered the interaction of class and education. He describes the changes in British schools which provide broader opportunities for continued education, and the attempts to equalize that opportunity across class lines. But he adds that the differentiation among types of secondary schools available—grammar, technical, and secondary modern—and the close link that education has to occupation in England has developed another social-class education dilemma.[29] The means for determining who goes to what school is a classification system based on tests of students, the results of which cause them to be sorted into different schools which offer different occupational, and thus social-class, preparation. Marshall states that the initial intent to equalize opportunity by permitting "the poor boy to show that he is as good as the rich boy" has, in the long run, simply redistributed inequalities. The classification by use of tests creates hierarchies which ignore differences among individuals within one class, and makes more explicit the differences between classes. Marshall takes the position that the advantage gained by opening educational opportunities which tend to eliminate status based on inherited privilege outweighs the disadvantage of creating an educational class system, but that the society should be aware of the fact that the link of education to occupation creates a system of social stratification despite the notions of equality inherent in free, open schools.[30]

Equality of opportunity in education in America has many of the components of the English system described by Marshall. Although the United States has had more broadly available schools and long ago lost the onus of "pauper schools" which was attached to public, free schools in contrast to upper-class private education, the inequalities of social position in America and the relation of education to occupation have provided some similar concerns. This has been particularly observable in the variance between black and white opportunities for education and jobs. One of the most significant investigations of this disparity in education is the government-sponsored $1.5 million study conducted by James Coleman

which found, among other interesting points, that school facilities, programs, teachers, and related quality of education indices were generally inferior in schools with predominantly black students. Although regional and specific school differences were noted, the general findings of disparity in opportunity for education held. Standardized achievement test data showed that average scores for black students were lower than those of other groups, and that the difference in mean scores between white and black students increased as the level of school increased. On tests of verbal and nonverbal skills, black students averaged 1.6 years below whites in the sixth grade, but by the twelfth grade the difference had doubled to 3.3 years. This increase in the difference between test scores is related to differences in the environment of youngsters, a large share of which is in the schools, and an apparently large share of which is the result of socioeconomic factors. The relation of social values and education is illustrated in results of the part of the Coleman study which measured attitudes and achievement. The data indicate that the achievement of whites was not significantly altered by being in a school with students of different educational aspirations, but that black students, and certain other minority groups, tended to have higher achievement when they were in schools with students who had higher educational aspirations.[31]

Patricia Cayo Sexton studied one large-city school system and "found that money spent on schools there, and the quality of education offered, varied in direct proportion to the income of families in the school neighborhood."[32] She found inequalities in virtually every aspect of the school environment and determined that these inequalities were correlated to school performance; students from lower-income families performed less well.[33] She concludes that, "In general, the more education one gets, the higher will be one's place in the stratification hierarchy."[34]

Linton and Nelson argue that,

> One of the most prominent avenues of social mobility in American society has been education. In early periods education was limited to an elite socioeconomic group. As democracy became more important as a social and political form, the need to educate larger segments of the population was acknowledged. . . . This tended to alter the concept of education as something worthy only of leisure classes. Practical education, public schools, compulsory attendance laws, and related popular education movements gained; the schools became a major force in social mobility.[35]

Summary

The school is influenced by and exerts influence on social class and mobility. The social structure is preserved and maintained in part by the schools through acceptance of the dominant social value system and inculcation of these values in youth. In America this amounts to education for middle-class citizenship almost regardless of the social-class origins of students. It has little impact on families in the upper strata since there are relatively few of them and they tend to use private finishing or preparatory schools. In the lower strata the imposition of middle-class values and the use of education as a tool for upward social mobility creates problems of aspiration attainment, alienation, dropouts, and *disadvantagement*. At the same time, the schools have provided a unifying force for the pluralism of American society. Education is an increasingly common opportunity and experience for each new generation. Yet we are faced with a conflict between the worthiness of education for stabilizing society by developing common attitudes and the need in a free society to educate for individual freedom and disparate social attitudes.

NOTES

1. Harold L. Hodgkinson, *Education, Interaction, and Social Change*, Prentice-Hall, Englewood Cliffs, N.J., 1967, pp. 89–97.
2. *Ibid.*, pp. 91–92.
3. Richard Centers, *The Psychology of Social Classes*, Princeton University Press, Princeton, N.J., 1949, as cited in Hodgkinson.
4. W. Lloyd Warner, *et al., Social Class in America*, Science Research, Chicago, 1949, chap. 2.
5. Joseph A. Kahl, *The American Class Structure*, Holt, Rinehart and Winston, New York, 1959.
6. Centers, p. 27.

7. *Ibid.*, pp. 76–77.
8. Harold L. Wilensky and Hugh Edwards, "The Skidder: Ideological Adjustments of Downward Mobile Workers," *American Sociological Review*, vol. 24, April, 1959, pp. 215–231.
9. A. Arnold Anderson, "A Skeptical Note on the Relation of Vertical Mobility to Education," *American Journal of Sociology*, vol. 66, May, 1961, pp. 560–570.
10. *Ibid.*
11. W. Lloyd Warner, Robert J. Havighurst and Martin B. Loeb, *Who Shall Be Educated?*, Harper & Row, New York, 1944.
12. August B. Hollingshead, *Elmtown's Youth*, Wiley, New York, 1949.
13. Robert J. Havighurst, "Social-Class Influences on American Education," from *Social Forces Influencing American Education*, Sixtieth Yearbook, Part 2, chap. v, National Society for the Study of Education, The University of Chicago Press, Chicago, 1961.
14. *Ibid.*, p. 121.
15. *Ibid.*
16. *Ibid.*, p. 122.
17. Robert J. Havighurst, "Problem Children and Social Class Differences in the Schools," in Thomas Linton and Jack L. Nelson, *Patterns of Power: Social Foundations of Education*, Pitman, New York, 1968, pp. 127–139.
18. *Ibid.*
19. W. Lloyd Warner, *Democracy in Jonesville*, Harper & Row, New York, 1949, pp. 194–196, 198–199.
20. *Ibid.*
21. *Ibid.*
22. W. W. Charters, Jr., "Social Class Analysis and the Control of Public Education," *Harvard Educational Review*, fall, 1953, pp. 268–283. See also Warner, Havighurst, and Loeb, *Who Shall Be Educated?*
23. Robert J. Havighurst and Bernice L. Neugarten, *Society and Education*, Allyn and Bacon, Boston, 1967, p. 395.
24. *Report of the National School Boards Association*, 1965, as reported in Patricia Cayo Sexton, *The American School: A Sociological Analysis*, Prentice-Hall, Englewood Cliffs, N.J., 1967, p. 29.
25. William M. Cave and Donald L. Halsted, "Sociology of Education," *Review of Educational Research*, vol. 37, February, 1967, pp. 74–81.
26. *Ibid.*, p. 76.
27. *Ibid.*, p. 78.
28. Thomas H. Marshall, *Class, Citizenship and Social Development*, Doubleday, Garden City, N.Y., 1964, p. 103.
29. *Ibid.*, p. 108.
30. *Ibid.*, pp. 107–110.
31. James S. Coleman, *et al.*, *Equality of Educational Opportunity*, U.S. Department of Health, Education, and Welfare, Office of Education, Government Printing Office, Washington, D.C., 1966.
32. Sexton, *The American School*, p. 38. In summary of Patricia C. Sexton, *Education and Income, Inequality of Opportunity in the Public Schools*, Viking, New York, 1961, p. 50.
33. *Ibid.*
34. *Ibid.*, p. 64.
35. Linton and Nelson, p. 67.

Chapter 10 / *The Schools: Structure and Functions*

As indicated previously, sociologists have several means available for analyzing social phenomena. One of several differing schools of thought in regard to understanding and explaining the institutions of society is that of *structural-functional analysis.* Structural-functional analysis considers the observable institutional framework and the manifest and latent functions assigned to and performed by the institution—in this case, education and, specifically, the schools. Because most readers have had considerable experience with the schools in one way or another, the treatment of structure and function given here is relatively succinct. We shall only sketch the formal structure of schools and comment on some of the functions of education in the American society.

There is much variation within the structure and function of American education. These differences are consistent with the nature of a pluralistic society but pose problems in discussing the overall institution of education in specific terms. Our presentation necessarily focuses on the general patterns of education—but not to the exclusion of atypical structural and functional occurrences.

Education is tied closely to its social milieu. Whether the schools lead or follow the society, they are potentially powerful institutions in any modern culture. Indeed education is a strong social agency in any culture, modern or primitive. The means of protecting ritual, ceremony, taboo, knowledge, art, music, mythology, or religion is essentially educational. Through learning methods of gathering and preparation of food, accumulation and disbursement of wealth, explanations of natural or supernatural phenomena, operation of the culture's social proprieties, and judgments about right and wrong, the child is socialized—and this is a form of education. Informal education continues throughout life. Man continues to learn, whether in a formally designed learning environment or not. In this sense, education and socialization are virtually synonymous.

This chapter, however, is limited to a consideration of formal education in a society. Formal education in schools, of course, is only one of many socialization agents. Newspapers, parents, peer groups, television, religion, unions, wives, neighbors, and gangs are only a few of the other agents. The schools, of course, are one of the most important socializing institutions in industrialized societies in that they provide a structured learning situation which may be continued for a prolonged period of time.

The Structure of Education

Education, as a major agent of socialization, is directly involved in the structure, functions, and values of the society in which it operates. It is a structural component in the sense that it is an institution of and for the society and is integrated with the society. In America, for example, formal education permeates the society at virtually every political and economic level. The battles over neighborhood schools, public financial aid to private schools, property taxes and lotteries for education, who should be admitted to prestige colleges, and integration of minority groups in schools, and other problems demonstrate the intertwining of education with social, political, and economic structures.

The Federal government has a large educational establishment operating from the Department of Health, Education and Welfare. The U.S. Office of Education and the Office of the Commissioner of Education are becoming increasingly important as larger amounts of funds are available for educational purposes. Each state has an executive officer for education, usually a state superintendent of schools, and a state department of education with some form of liaison with the governor's office and the legislature. Every village, town, suburb, or city is within the structural boundaries of school systems of one sort or another. Scarcely an area exists in the country that is not formally within the structural framework of education.

The Federal Government and Education

Education is big business today. In the United States, government expenditure for formal education has increased steadily since World War II and is now approximately $60 billion per year. Of this amount about $35 billion is spent on public schools, $5 billion on private schools, and the remainder on higher education. The Federal government, through grants of land and money for school operation, building, and research, contributes between 5 and 10 percent of this money, and state and local governments provide the rest. In the typical community the public school budget is as large as that of major industries of the area. At the Federal level the cost of education does not compare with the cost of defense, but it has become a considerable portion of the budget for domestic affairs.[1]

Although there has been Federal assistance to education ever since the Northwest Ordinance of 1787, the major push toward Federal support of schools has come in recent times. The land grants for education contained in the Northwest Ordinance and in later laws like the Morrill Act of 1862 (which created land grant colleges) gave way to money grants to institutions and to scholars. The Federal influence on education through financial support became pronounced with the G.I. Bills, the National Defense Education Act of 1958, and the Elementary and Secondary Education Act of 1965. The administration of these and other Federal financial support bills has enlarged the scope and power of the U.S. Office of Education and related Federal agencies.

Despite the increasing role of the Federal government in education, the significant structure of schools remains a state enterprise in the United States, largely because of historical and legal considerations. At the time of the Constitutional Convention schools were essentially privately owned or state-controlled. The U.S. Constitution contains no statement about education, and the Tenth Amendment provides that the states retain control over all areas not specifically designated for Federal control. The result has been the development of strong state and local systems of education with power vested in state constitutions, legislatures, and boards of education. At the Federal level the main educational concerns have been expressed through operation of schools in U.S. protectorates, foreign countries, and Indian schools, plus provisions for Federal financial assistance to schools through such programs as school lunches, vocational training, the G.I. Bill, and educational research.

In addition, the Federal government, through the Supreme Court, has taken legal action on Constitutional grounds in such cases as church-state separation on school aid, segregation of black students in schools, pledging allegiance to the flag, and loyalty oaths required of teachers. The grounds for Federal involvement in these matters rest in the "general welfare" clause of the Constitution and the guarantees granted in the Bill of Rights. The Fourteenth Amendment has been of considerable use in permitting the Federal government to intercede in order to assure equal education to minority groups. The 1954 decision of the Supreme Court, which altered an earlier court decision on separate but equal education for Negroes, is a good example of the Federal government's interest in the formal structure of education. The resulting order to desegregate schools has had dramatic social and educational impact throughout the country. It also illustrates one of the problems in the educational structure of the country. Since there is no Federal power to require states to operate public schools and since the states have the power to control education, the desegregation decision has been difficult to enforce. Proponents of states' rights have fought those who believe in Federal surveillance of individual rights on this issue.

Another example of increasing Federal involvement through the educational structure is the poverty programs. Here, as in integration, the schools are used as social reform agencies. One of the most prominent themes in the poverty programs has been to promote educational programs. Some of these are designed to teach skills to the unemployed to help them find employment, some to increase literacy, and some to train social workers to go into poverty areas. Each of these programs uses the education structure, either through the development of school programs for the disadvantaged persons or through higher educational programs to train people to work with them. One new development is that Federal funds are being utilized by industries of various types to offer special training and education for youth outside the formal school system.

The two most prominent themes in Federal financial aid to schools have been that (1) schools are important to the country as means of social reform, and (2) schools are important as means of national defense and security.

The social reform theme is demonstrated by activities in the poverty, deprivation, and segregation areas. The national security interest is shown by the requirement of military training contained in the Morrill Act, and the reaction to Sputnik in 1957 which triggered the National Defense Education Act of 1958.

State Structure and Education

Many textbooks on educational administration stress that, although the Federal government should be interested in education, the schools remain a function of each state and the responsibility of each local school district. This view is oversimplified, but it expresses the legal framework for the operation of schools. The states retain legal control of schools and are jealous of attempts to interfere with their control. The authority to establish and maintain schools is delegated to the local districts, but the state remains powerful in such areas as school accreditation, teacher certification, financial support, general curriculum guidelines, school budgeting and auditing and school building design.

Most states have constitutional provisions regarding education. These provisions may vary from statements guaranteeing common schools for all to minimum salaries for teachers. State constitutions normally provide an overall structure for education by vesting authority in particular bodies such as the legislature and the state board of education. Usually the details of school structure within the state are expressed in statutory laws enacted by the state legislature and the regulations of the state board. The state executive officer of education, elected in some states and appointed in others, has advisory powers to the state board and operates the state education establishment through some form of state education department.

County, city, and local school districts are operated as arms of the state education bureau. Local school boards are the delegated authority to establish local policy so long as their policy falls within the guidelines determined by the state. The local district is semiautonomous in determining its budget, school building, curriculum, teaching materials, and hiring and firing policies, but the state usually retains surveillance and sanction rights, including the registration of programs and personnel, budget restrictions, and state-approved teaching materials. State imposition of authority varies according to the legal structure, history, and personalities of each state. In some states teaching materials are selected by state textbook committees; in some the curriculum is largely state controlled; and in some the tax structure for support of schools is rigidly established.

There are, however, many areas in which the local school system has almost complete control. Teacher salaries and teaching loads, facilities and equipment for schools, determination of some curricula and materials, and internal structure of the schools may all be determined by the individual school district. At the local level the formal structure normally consists of an elected or appointed board of education, a superintendent appointed by them, and a staff of administrators and teachers. Districts, of course, vary in complexity of bureaucracy from rural, one-room, one-teacher schools supervised by a county or state education agency to complex systems in major urban areas with thousands of teachers and a vast network of central administrative offices separating the classroom activity from the school superintendent.

Functions of Education

Education has social, political, and economic tasks consistent with its socialization role. It has been given some functions and forced into others. Such tasks as conveying the accumulated wisdom of the culture are basic to the function of education in a society; indeed they form the cultural-transmission role of education discussed previously. The schools are supposed to transmit the cultural heritage to the young. A definition of the content of cultural heritage varies from country to country and school to school. Some areas constrain the schools to purely academic transmission of information; others view the school as a subsociety and demand that schools undertake transmission of leisure time, vocational, and social protocol activities. Thus schools may have bowling and cake-decorating, business and industrial arts, home economics, etiquette, and driver education classes.

There are a number of other functions of education in society which show the relationship of the schools to the structure and values of the culture. The following listing is suggestive, not complete. Interrelated functions are separated only for analytical purposes.

1. *The school as a behavior modifier.* Because of our Puritan tradition in education, and the supplemental work of psychologists in analyzing learning, the school has accepted the function of modifying the behavior of youngsters. The Puritans were concerned that the evil inherent in man should be controlled, and their schools were used to control children and require that they be good.

The Calvinistic tradition which required suppression of evil thoughts and behaviors was a dominant influence on early schools in America. Not only was strict religious morality a primary theme in teaching materials, teachers and parents were expected to exert physical control over the behavior of youngsters. This is evident in drawings of schoolmasters, punishment utensils, and schoolrooms of the period. The authority role still in existence in teachers and schools draws from this tradition. School requirements on student dress, hair styles, raising hands before speaking, orderliness, lining up single file, no speaking in study halls, obedience and docility are part of this concept of behavior modification. These are behaviors which do not occur naturally in children, but are part of the moral history from Puritan ideas on child rearing.

The work of learning psychologists, who may not be in accord with Puritan concepts of evil and control, still contributed to the school's function in behavior modification. Studies in behaviorism led to means of controlling behavior. Learning is often defined as a change in behavior, and the behavioral psychologist looks for this change as a measure of learning. The current emphasis on cognitive learning, behavioral school objectives, and successful manipulation of student behaviors in programed instruction has gained advocates in the schools.

Often the behavioral psychologists decry some aspects of what is done in schools to modify student behavior, just as the moralists decry some aspects of what is done in behavioral teachings. The combination of these two, however, has enhanced behavior modification as a major function of schools. Education has developed into an institution for moral as well as intellectual behavior modification.

From kindergarten on, children learn social behavior toward other children and the teacher. Sharing, playing together, obeying the teacher, cleaning up the room, using the correct signals to request bathroom time, regulating activities by the clock, repressing strong emotions, being quiet, limiting physical violence, and smiling on cue are examples of behavior expectations imposed by schools. In later school years the student learns such behaviors as opening a book properly, using the library card catalog, reading and writing, cheating on tests, translating known objects into abstract numbers, unacceptable language, dating, sportsmanship, and technical skills like typing.

The school, of course, is not the only avenue for learning these behaviors, but it has considerable influence in the shaping of moral and intellectual actions of the youth in a society. Sometimes the modification of behavior toward socially approved patterns in a socially sensitive institution like schools is obtained at the sacrifice of some other beneficial behaviors. Consider the creative child. If he were permitted sufficient freedom to express his creativity and individualism, he might make outstanding contributions to mankind. But often principals and teachers feel threatened by creative youngsters who do not adapt to the school environment. The child's behavior is modified when he is forced to conform to standard school patterns. While social conformity operates smoothly for the majority of children in schools because they have experienced it in families and peer groups earlier, it poses distinct problems for children, creative or not, who have had widely differing socialization patterns. Individualism is sacrificed to social control in most of these cases, but sometimes creative talent is also sacrificed.

2. *The school as a purifier*. From crime to drug addiction to birth control, the school has been viewed as a means for solving society's ills. Many observers insist that the school is capable of preventing crime, sex deviation, drug addiction, poor driving, over-population, and air-pollution, and that it can rehabilitate deviants. Although this function is related to behavior modification, it exists as a major part of much of the rhetoric surrounding the values of education. The schools are initial targets of campaigns to improve society by wiping out prejudice, want, poverty, injustice, inequality, delinquency, and immorality. Even among those who see that the schools usually are not in a position to make revolutionary changes in society, there is a revisionist zeal which supports the school as an agent of social improvement. This zeal for purification has caused schools to initiate and develop a vast array of special programs and activities from psychological services to school breakfasts.

3. *The school as a marriage bureau*. Because of the coeducational structure of schools, their ubiquitousness, and of course, the age of their students, schools often serve as the present-day "matchmaker." When adolescents of both sexes share in the same building, classes, and social activities for relatively long periods of time, it is natural that the school becomes an arena for courting.

4. *The school as a sorting agency*. The educational system can be pictured as a machine with a large hopper at the top, dials and gauges in the midsection, and a series of outlet tubes spreading below into various separate baskets. Into the hopper is fed the raw material: children. As they progress through the dials and gauges of the enclosed box (the school), they are pulled, pushed, and squeezed into channels leading to specific outlet tubes. The resulting product is spewed into different baskets marked *blue collar, white collar, sales, managerial, professional, reject*, and so forth. This describes the sorting function of education. Obviously, it is not a perfect analogy, and it does not allow for the student's efforts toward determining his own goal, but it does show a simplified model of operation. The school tends to sort people occupationally, economically, and socially. The socioeconomic aspect of sorting was discussed

in Chapter 9; discussion here will center upon the occupational "out-baskets."

Occupational sorting provides several functions for the society. Students select vocational preparation programs with the help of teachers, counselors, and parents. Schools provide vocational counseling as well as actual training programs, adult education courses, and related activities. Counselors also make vocational selections for students by assigning them to specific curricula according to test scores and grades.

The schools also serve other occupational purposes. They provide the necessary credentials, varying from the high school diploma needed for a blue-collar position to the Ph.D. needed by the college professor. In the United States education has become one of the main criteria for employment. A reading of help-wanted advertisements provides ample evidence of the influence of education on occupational sorting. Educational requirements are seldom waived for job applicants. The police force demands high school preparation for employment and often college work to be promoted. Business determines educational requirements for particular kinds of employment, and the rough-hewn, hard-working person who attains an executive position without a college degree is becoming increasingly rare. Almost all college teachers must have a doctorate. It took academic courage for the University of California to appoint Eric Hoffer, the philosopher-longshoreman, to a research position. Hoffer had not been to school even at the elementary level, but was a self-taught scholar.

?

Teachers

The schools also provide employers with a means of controlling the supply of applicants. Any employer can limit the number of applicants for a position by altering the educational requirements. This is also true of some professions, like medicine and law, which use the educational system as a means of controlling the number of practitioners. Since schools evaluate the presumed capacities and achievements of the young, they serve as efficient occupational sorting agents. They may not, however, serve society well in that the educational cut off point may be determined more by factors of supply and demand than by the overall quality of the applicants.

5. *The school as parental substitute.* The legal term, *in loco parentis,* refers to the school's acting *in place of the parent.* A number of court cases have determined that the school has this function; and civil action can be brought against the school board, administrators, and teachers for being negligent in this role. Schools which utilize forms of corporal punishment have used this role as a legal protection. The function of parental substitution may be performed in a number of ways, including continual supervision of students while at school; requirements for nutritious meals in the school cafeteria; censorship of certain books, films, and other materials; baby-sitting activities; requirements of manner and dress; and imposition of the school's authority on the student.

Parents, in general, approve of the school's role of substitution, so long as it does not conflict dramatically with home patterns. Assistance with toilet training at the lower levels and discipline at the higher levels is usually appreciated. Many parents even view the schools simply as a socially approved place to leave their children. They may be unconcerned with what goes on at school and become irate when school closes unexpectedly because of bad weather and they are forced to have their children at home.

Other roles of schools as parental substitutes are demonstrated in the curriculum. Sex education is a growing movement, and many schools take heavy responsibilities in this regard. Driver education has been mentioned before, but is a fine example of parental substitution. Health and hygiene courses, cooking, sewing, woodworking and other classes are similar examples.

6. *The schools as conveyors of mass values.* Education is an ideal means for maintaining social norms. It offers a close-knit, organized structure, the school, which has large segments of the population under social surveillance for long periods of time. Whether public or private, schools operate under society's watchful eye, and the ability of a school to be at variance with the norms of its social constituency is severely limited. In addition, peer groups exert considerable normative pressure on individuals, and schools provide an excellent setting for this

influence. Fads abound in schools, and those who deviate from them are often mocked or even ostracized. The competition to be among the "in" group causes students to succumb to a variety of school subculture pressures. Both the school's reflection of local social norms and the student's acceptance of peer group norms are illustrative of the function of schools as conveyors of mass values. Individualism, supposedly sought after in American society, is often overwhelmed by the educational system.

The schools have evolved a cult of conformity which acts upon the student in several ways beyond peer group pressure. Teachers, counselors, principals, board members, and the PTA tend to demand model students with model behavior. The good student is defined in two dimensions: intellectual and moral. He is expected to be responsible as well as intelligent. It is hard to conceive of a school honoring its most creative student despite the fact that he had cut classes, was tardy, refused counseling, and was an intellectual threat to the teachers. The conformity that schools express in expecting model behavior is also demonstrated in curricula which establish and promote model attitudes.

Determination of what subjects are good for all students, and thus should be required, has consumed much educational literature and curriculum-committee time. It is assumed that required courses are in the interests of a society. Such required courses or required classroom materials are expected to provide equal opportunity for enlightenment. Selection of common textbooks, course outlines, and examinations promotes curricular conformity despite continuing educational discourse on providing for individual differences.

Model attitudes are fostered through the relatively conservative social morality of teachers, textbook publishers, and concerned parents. A middle-class morality pervades schools and maintains a value system similar to the Puritan ethic in its attitudes toward hard work, frugality, virtue, chastity, humility, reverence, moderation, and honesty. Students constantly hear these social attitudes from school personnel, teaching materials, and the vocal public. The student who is able to understand complex abstractions without obvious hard work in class or at home is viewed skeptically. He will be required to remain in class the full time and to complete all meaningless homework regardless of his mental prowess.

The result of this function of schools as conveyors of mass values and norms is to create successful conformists as well as social deviates. It also serves the socialization process by conveying real models of social success and failure based on accumulation of wealth, physical power, popularity, and conformity in addition to the socially acceptable models described earlier.

7. *The school as an agent for nationalism.* Every country utilizes its school system for the development of national spirit and patriotism in its youth. This function of education is one of the most broadly developed of the various roles played by the schools. Nearly all national committees which draft purposes and goals of education have agreed that the production of citizens for the nation is a major goal. Modern industrialized countries use the schools as agencies of nationalism in forms varying from strongly overt to relatively subtle. Nazi Germany is the obvious example of an education system operated for the proclaimed national interest without respect to scholarship, intellectual inquiry, or freedom. Teachers and teaching materials which did not conform to the Nazi model were eliminated from the system. The same nationalistic educational phenomena, usually more subtle or less restrictive, are found in virtually all countries. National goals are expressed as educational goals. This was as true in ancient Sparta and Athens as it is today.

Practical school considerations are also infused with a national ideology. Each country requires study of its own history, government, and literature, normally expressed in very positive terms. National heroes, writers, and politicians are treated well in the schools. Teachers are often screened for political views; teaching materials convey only the correct national image; national rituals of song, dance, and loyalty pervade the schools; and instruction which is felt to be inimical to national spirit is grounds for action against the schools.

State

The United States supplies numerous examples of nationalism in education. Loyalty oaths required of teachers before they will be employed is a prime example. State regulations and curricula which require courses designed to show the superiority of the American governmental and economic system over others are another illustration. Censorship of text materials by school boards, curriculum committees, and administrators occurs in a large number of schools, and publishers may refuse to publish unpatriotic materials. This is normally in response to reactions by patriotic organizations which exert public pressure on the schools and book publishers. Other examples of nationalism in American schools are pledging allegiance to the flag, singing the National Anthem, celebrating the birthdays of Washington and Lincoln, and taking courses in American history.

The justification for nationalism in education is that political socialization is an important aspect of any country and cannot be ignored without possible loss of national identity. Since citizenship implies national ties, it would be strange to assume that the schools could educate for citizenship without promoting national pride and patriotism. A second rationale posed by advocates of more nationalistic education is that of competition with other nations. If one country educates for internationalism while its opponents continue nationalistic school training, there is a presumed threat to national security. Thus it is argued, preservation of the nation rests on the ability of the schools to persuade youngsters of the national values. In any case, the schools have a nationalistic function.

Summary

Schools are dynamic institutions which share in performing the functions of a society. The allocation of these functions, the operation of them, and the structure for performing them are constantly in change, yet have degrees of permanence.

Schools are conservative bureaucracies, generally reflecting prior social norms, organizational patterns, and functions. At the same time, schools in mass education societies have the potential for social restruction or destruction. This chapter has not exhausted the possibilities in school structure or function, but has exemplified common practices over a period of time.

NOTES

1. Department of Health, Education and Welfare, *Fall, 1968 Statistics of Public Schools*, Office of Education, Government Printing Office, Washington, D.C., 1968.
2. U.S. Department of Commerce, Bureau of the Census, *Statistical Abstract of the United States, 1969*, U.S. Government Printing Office, 1969.

Chapter 11 / *The Self-Concept, Segregation, and the School*

Development of the Self-Concept

Within the past few years, sociological analysis of human behavior has placed increasing emphasis on the *self-concept*. The construct has not been well-defined in most cases, but generally refers to the way in which an individual views himself, that is, how does he define himself—for example, good athlete, bad boy. This self-concept does not exist in a vacuum. The individual defines himself only in relation to the objects and people around him. Thus as a child progresses through his environment, the people and objects with which he comes in contact help him to develop a definition of himself. For example, the traditional Japanese boy is told by word and action to be aggressive in his dealings both with peers and female adult members of the family. The girl, on the other hand, is told by word and action to be submissive, particularly to the male members of the family, even those who are younger than she is. These presented definitions lead to self-concepts: the Japanese boy considers himself brave, aggressive, and forthright, while the Japanese woman considers herself demure, shy, and stylized. For each of us, the most important parts of the definition of self are presented by the most important people in our lives, the *significant others.* These are the people whose opinion matters most. With children they are usually adult members of the family—parents, grandparents, etc.

The construct of importance here is that the self-concept is directly related to behavior; that is, the way in which we define ourselves in relation to our society will in many ways determine how we react to that society. For example, the child who has been programed into one remedial class after another will eventually develop a negative self-concept with regard to his learning ability. When he comes to believe that he is incapable of learning, no amount of academic help can make him learn. The first task would be to prove to him that he is capable of learning at all. Another example is the child who is constantly told by his teachers, "We are watching you because you have a record of bad behavior." The chances are that such a child will continue his bad behavior even if he might originally have wished to end it.

The examples are endless, but the construct is quite simple: (1) significant others present us with a set of definitions of how we relate to our society; (2) as these definitions are incorporated into our life style, they become part of our self-concept; and (3) our self-concept in large part determines how we react to the actions of our society. A classic example is the social worker and the prostitute walking down the same street; even though the street is the same, they will see different things because they define the environment differently.

What happens to a child in school is important to the development of his self-concept. In the first place, he spends six to eight hours a day there. This is more than he spends in any single waking activity. Second, as discussed previously, our society has placed great emphasis upon the school, both for the intrinsic importance of education and as a method of maintaining or improving socioeconomic status. The school, in brief, is one of the significant others in the life of the child. Depending on his self-concept, the child can react in one of three ways to the school and its regimen. If the child has a positive self-concept, there is a great likelihood that he will do well academically and have little difficulty adjusting to the regimen of the school. If he has a negative self-concept he will probably do badly in school academically but have too little strength to be a discipline problem. If, on the other hand, he has no self-concept at all, if he is in a state of normlessness or *anomie*, or if his self-concept disregards the school's definitions, then he will tend to strike out at the school and flout academic and disciplinary rules. It is significant that in the recent riots those black youths who had a negative self-image were not involved since they felt that they were incapable of doing anything. Primarily involved were those who had a positive self-concept but were frustrated ("I could make it if the ofays would only let me") or those who had absolutely nothing to lose except their lack of identity ("At least now they know we are here").

Black Self-Concepts

One of the basic difficulties in any discussion of black self-concept has been to dispel the idea that it is formed in ways significantly different from that of any other person. There seems to be the feeling among many, particularly white, citizens that different forces operate on black people. This is obviously and patently false. If the black child has positive significant others with whom to identify, he will have a positive self-image; if he has negative others with whom to identify, he will have a negative self-concept; if he has nothing with which to identify or if he feels that the significant others are "nonpeople," he will lack a self-concept. If we assume that self-concepts are formed in direct relationship to the significant others in our life spheres, then we must also assume that white and black children form self-concepts in the same way.

One principal difference between the black and white child is that the white child has an historical perspective, a racial heritage. It is not that the white child has so much to be proud of; indeed most white children have very little concept of race. Rather, this child has no negative feelings about his own race. He assumes from his parents an historical tradition. The black child has not been allowed to feel himself part of an historical progression.

As Kardiner and Ovesey have pointed out, when the slaves arrived on these shores, they retained little of their African culture. For example, members of the same tribe, the same religious tradition, or the same family group were rarely sold to the same master. Furthermore, much of the African culture was no longer relevant. The American Negro was "culture-stripped." This distinguishes him from the African counterpart who is part of an historical tradition, regardless of how primitive or cosmopolitan that African culture may appear now. It is a culture, and the children are brought up within a tradition.

Kardiner and Ovesey list six imperatives for the continuance of a culture and point out how each of these was denied the slave. Their imperatives are:

1. There must be sufficient numbers to propagate the culture. This does not mean only that there be procreation but also that the cultural patterns of procreation be maintained; that is, that the family tribal and cultural units be maintained.
2. The cultural institutions must be relevant to the situation of the group; that is, the culture which the slaves brought with them from Africa had to be relevant to their new status in the New World.
3. Norms and role status must be continued so that cooperation and coordination of labor can continue. For example, the African tribes were primarily patriarchal, and for the culture to continue, this male-centered family unit would have to continue.
4. A balance must be maintained between frustration and gratification; that is, when there is frustration there must be a corresponding method of attaining gratification.

5. Each constituent must be granted access to the wider societal norms; there must be communication between the individual and the culture which surrounds him. This is not so much to say that every person must have direct contact with the entire culture, but rather that he must have the feeling that the entire culture is open to his advances, that within the realm of the culture he will be allowed to communicate.
6. There must be reciprocal emotional interaction between the various members of the society. Here the problem is not so much that there be communication but rather that the communication be positive and that the communication be between equals.

As Kardiner and Ovesey point out, when the slaves arrived they lost all six of these mandates of culture. If the destruction of the original culture had coincided with access to the master's culture, however, the slaves would not have been much worse for the experience. For example, during certain periods, the Romans had slaves and the original culture of the slaves was also broken down. The Romans, however, supplanted the original culture with their own. An extraordinary instance is Epictetus who was born a slave but rose to the position of a great philosopher in the Roman culture. The American pattern of slavery, on the other hand, both destroyed the original culture and then denied the slave access to the patterns of the master. Here were the beginnings not so much of a negative self-concept as of the lack of any self-concept which had relevance to the slave. Furthermore, whereas freed slaves in other cultures were allowed to enter the main stream of the dominant culture, the freed slaves in the United States were, if anything, further removed from the central societal patterns.

This pattern of denial has not been muted by the passage of time. The black child is still denied a relevant self-concept. He feels outnumbered and overpowered by the white power structure; he feels that the institutions of the society are not relevant to his existence; he feels that his status as a human being as well as an American is destroyed every time he attempts to get a job or buy a house or join a union; his frustrations far outnumber his gratifications. He feels that the police, the realtors, the schools, and the churches are all white structures designed to keep him in his place. He feels that he has no recourse, that he has no place to which he can turn. His access to the overall culture is extremely limited. The black child goes to schools which are overwhelmingly segregated, as is his neighborhood, his future occupational status, and his life. He never knows what the emotional reaction to him will be. One white person will treat him with contempt while another will treat him with kindness for the same act. Furthermore if he becomes aggressive in his demands for equality, then the white world calls him an agitator or a "black militant" fanatic. If he retreats and sulks, he is called petulant. If he smiles, he is called a "good nigger" which means one who has accepted the projection of the white world as his own self-concept.

We have, then, a situation which distinguishes the black from the white child; namely, that the white child has been allowed a history while the black child has not. When this is combined with the constant reminders that he is really not part of the overall culture and that he, because of his race, is not worthwhile, it should not be surprising to find so many black ghetto children who have weak or almost nonexistent egos.

Another major classification aside from that of weak or nonexistent egos is that of children with negative self-concepts. Some of the dynamics here are similar to those which build the lack of self-concept; however, the resultant personality is quite different. The difference is between "I am black and that is evil," and James Baldwin's "I am black and *Nobody Knows My Name*." As Clark and Clark have pointed out, black children understand that they are black and that it is better to be white. When black children were presented with brown and white dolls and asked which doll was better ("Which would you rather play with," "which is nicest,") they picked the white doll. When they were asked which doll was more like themselves, they picked the brown doll. Admittedly this study is not a recent one (1940–1941), but the same dynamics still hold; everything within the society tells the black child that it is better to be white than black. His parents live in inferior housing, have inferior jobs, have been taught to think that they have inferior folk heroes, are not taught about their own people in school or the place of the Negro in American culture, and so forth.

Within the school itself the Negro child is presented with the idea that his home, his family, his neighborhood, and his "self" are not worthy. The school presents him with a set of middle-class white standards, norms, and rules. He is expected to be well-dressed (actually the opposite is sometimes true, since many teachers in an attempt to be tolerant tell black students that they know that their parents are not capable of supporting them as white parents would), punctual even though punctuality may be neither necessary nor possible in a slum environment (the students are usually punished for tardiness rather than retrained), to eat well (even though inferior stores in their slum area may make that impossible), and so forth. Furthermore the black student sees the greatest turnover in teachers since most teachers do not wish to teach in slum situations.

The combination of living in a slum, of seeing his parents degraded, of seeing his father driven from the central place in the family by his inability and his mother's ability to find work, by the menial type of work which he sees his fellow blacks forced to take if they are to work at all, and the insidious (albeit unintended) prejudices of the schools—this combination can lead to little else but a negative self-concept.

Until recently, there were only three choices open to the black child: (1) withdraw into no self-concept, accept no definition of the self; (2) accept the white man's definition and develop a negative self-concept; or (3) adopt the white man's mores and become a black bourgeois. This last alternative is difficult since it means that he must alienate himself almost completely from his present environment. This is the difficulty of so many bright black children who are faced with the hostility of their peers if they adopt this white culture and at the same time are not at all sure that they will be welcomed by the white world if they do adopt it. This position takes great strength of character (in terms of facing an unknown future) or such great alienation (from the present slum culture) that the choice is seldom made.

Of late, however, a new choice has become available to the black child. This choice is to develop a positive self-concept, not through pride in individual accomplishments, but rather through pride in racial accomplishments. There is a growing feeling among many young blacks that they are no longer alone in their struggle. And not only is there a feeling that other blacks will help and defend them, but that there are historical figures about whom they can be proud: Toussaint L'Ouverture, Frederick Douglass, Crispus Attucks, and many others. Furthermore, there is a growing feeling that what they as a race have accomplished during the last fifteen years was not done for them by whites but was done by themselves through their own leaders. There is a growing feeling that the black revolution is part of a longer tradition of black dissidence, self-reliance, and greatness.

Accompanying this feeling of history, however, is the feeling that the white power structure neither understands nor wishes to know about this history. There is too much George Washington Carver and Booker T. Washington and not enough W. E. B. Du Bois (who particularly in his early years was one of the truly great sociologists of the United States) and Frederick Douglass. There is a growing demand on the part of blacks that their children be allowed to learn in the schools about their own heroes and their own history. This can even be carried one step further: there is every reason to believe that the African cultures of the Gold and Ivory Coasts were at a very high level indeed when slaves were brought to the United States. Demands that both black and white children know more about this tradition have been increasing. The basic argument seems to be that if the white child is asked to learn about the white Anglo-Saxon tradition, then both the white and the black child should learn about the African culture. The primary argument however, should be that the introduction of this type of material will increase the understanding and appreciation of both black and white children for each other, and automatically will increase the black child's sense of belonging to an historical tradition and thereby, his positive self-image.

Building a positive self-image does not, however, occur only through the introduction of an historical background. There must also be present-day figures with whom the child can identify. First and foremost, of course, there must be a greater emphasis upon the stability of positive male models for the child to follow; that is, the family must be stable and the father must maintain his traditional American role as breadwinner and protector. Not only is there a great concern with this problem in the white power structure, but there is also a growing concern in the black community itself and especially among black males. Furthermore, as businesses, unions, and professions become increasingly open to black workers, there will be a greater opportunity for the black male to assume his paternal role.

Of course, even a stable family would not be enough if there were nothing to be proud of outside of the family. This would only lead to a generalized alienation from the rest of the race. What is needed are living heroes who are seen and spoken to by the children. The last 15 years have seen a great number of these leaders, most of whom the white world does not understand.

The white world seems to feel that Stokely Carmichael speaks only for a fringe group of fanatics. This was even more true of its attitude toward Malcolm X, who was saying to his fellow blacks "Be proud that you are black. Be proud of your accomplishments. Be proud that you can scare the white world into giving you freedom. Be proud that you are forced to fight for what you have and what you will have and that the white world gives nothing out of the goodness of its heart." Malcolm X gave his listeners the feeling that they were worthwhile human beings, that they could have a positive self-image if they would only stop believing what the white world said about them. That the Muslims had great influence over blacks and that they were capable of developing positive self-images among their converts is perhaps best pointed out by their magnificent record in the treatment and cure of drug addicts, prostitutes, and alcoholics. They have said, "Be proud and you won't need to take dope."

The School's Relation to the Positive Black Self-Concept

What, in effect, is happening is that the black child is developing a positive racial self-image, albeit at the expense of the white world's image. The question which faces educators is whether or not it is necessary for a black child to develop a negative concept of the white world before he can develop a positive concept of himself. Most people, of course, hope that it is not necessary. But unless the schools take a far more active role in the creation of this positive self-concept, the black child will be left with few alternatives. What the school must do is clear, although its actually doing it is often far more difficult. First and foremost, the school must take its rightful place as the educational leader in the community. For far too long the schools have allowed themselves to be bullied and badgered by power groups within the local or national community and have placed political expediency above educational soundness and democratic principles.

There are few, if any, educators who would be willing to say that in the long run there is any educational or democratic reason for maintaining a policy of racial segregation; either intentional or unintentional. Schools must integrate. This is not only because ghetto schools are inferior (and this has been proven over and over again in one study after another) but also because of the evils of segregation with regard to the self-concept of the black child. The longer he is segregated, the more he will feel that the segregation is legitimate or at least necessary. Furthermore this child is again excluded from the wider society. If this exclusion is allowed to continue, then society must be prepared to weather more riots which are bred out of the frustration of being "separate but equal."

Segregation breeds either a negative self-concept or an alienation which will lead to an estrangement from the greater society.

There is, however, one further evil of segregation which is seldom mentioned; if the white child is to learn to live in a cosmopolitan world, he cannot afford ignorance or prejudice. Nor will he be able to afford the shock when he meets a black African over a conference table or at an international business meeting. During his formative years he must learn to accept others as they are without the feeling of being "tolerant" or tolerating the other. There is only one way to learn acceptance, and that is through personal contact. If the Caucasian child has never come face to face with anyone outside of his own group, he will be that much less able to meet the complex world in which he must live.

Both the black and the white child need to be presented with accurate information about the history and traditions of the black people both here in the United States and in Africa. The present plans which include separate sections on Negro history are missing the point since they again contain the implicit assumption that black history is separate from white history. The thing which the school still has not recognized is that the black student is an American and that his history is just as much a part of American history as is English, German, or Polish history. Further, the great black thinkers and leaders of the past and the present are not separate but an integral part of the flow of historical thought of this country. The day of dividing history into American and Negro-American must end in favor of the inclusion of the history of all Americans in courses and curricula.

The basic point of this chapter is that it is important for the black child to develop a positive self-concept. The school's role in this development can take one of two directions. First, it can attempt to give black and white children different but equally positive identities. This would necessitate an increase in segregation. Second, it can bring both black and white children fully and completely into the total American culture by eliminating racial segregation in the schools. The easiest way to do this would be to integrate housing, but this probably will not happen until both the black and white children of this generation are free from the bigotries of their parents. It may be that the only way the school can aid in this process is by integrating its facilities with deliberate haste. It may even be that as parents see that their children can play together, they will learn to live together in the same neighborhoods.

BIBLIOGRAPHY

Baldwin, James, *Nobody Knows My Name*, Dell, New York, 1954.
Baldwin, James, *Notes on a Native Son*, Beacon Press, Boston, 1949.
Karatacius, William C., *Negro Self Concept*, McGraw-Hill, New York, 1965.
Kardiner, Abram, and Lionel Ovesey, *The Mark of Oppression*, Meridian Books, World Publishing, Cleveland, 1962, xix, 396.
Clark, Kenneth B. and Mamie D. Clark, "Racial Identification and Preference in Negro Children," in Eleanor E. Maccoby, Theodore M. Newcomb, and Eugene L. Hartley, *Readings in Social Psychology*, Holt, Rinehart and Winston, New York, 1958.
Malcolm X, *Autobiography of Malcolm X*, Grove Press, New York, 1966.
Wright, Richard, *Native Son*, Signet Books, New York, 1961.

Chapter 12 / *The Teacher in Society*

The teacher's status, role, and function in society depend upon the specific time and culture. Although there are no certain generalizations about society's view of teachers, there is some consensus about the status normally ascribed to teachers, the role in society which they are expected to play, and the particular functions which they normally perform.

To gain insight into several of these variables, one has only to consider archetypes of teachers and their implications. The following examples illustrate varying perceptions of well-known teachers.

Socrates, as known through Plato, is generally viewed as a wise man, a seeker of truth, a believer in freedom, a stimulator of curiosity, and a model of courage. Although a controversial figure in his own society, he had great social status and esteem and has continued to be a model for classroom discourse.

Ichabod Crane, schoolmaster in Washington Irving's tale, is the stereotype of a bumbling, oafish, narrow-minded teacher who deserves the scapegoat role he receives.

Mr. Chips, from James Hilton's *Good-bye Mister Chips*, is the image of the beloved, dedicated, kindly teacher who has little money, but is rich in spirit and an inspiration for his students.

Our Miss Brooks, of radio and early television fame, is feather-headed, capable of practical jokes, lovable and vital, but unrelated to reality and scarcely intellectual.

Mr. Novak, of the National Education Association–advised television series is a suave, personable teacher who is very competent in the classroom and in human relations.

Each of these teacher-types has some parallel in the schools of contemporary society. If a word-association test were given in which *teacher* was a cue word, the response would probably include attributes described above. Recollections of one's own teachers vary along these same lines. Since status is influenced by perceptions of the society in regard to role and function, any generally held view of teachers and teaching will have an impact on the role performance of teachers and on the selection of teaching as a career. If teaching as a profession is typically viewed as socially negative, it will not recruit talented youth, and those persons who are teachers will tend to conform to behavior patterns consistent with their social status. If teaching is viewed positively, teachers will tend to be of high caliber. Teaching has been associated with high and low social statuses in its past.

Even within the teaching field, perceptions of social status differ greatly. Often, a teacher's status varies according to the grade level he teaches. Although the disparity has been altered considerably as a result of increased educational requirements for all teachers and a relatively uniform income among teachers of elementary and secondary schools, there is still a great discrepancy in status among elementary-school, secondary-school, and college teachers. This is partly the result of historic precedent, level of educational attainment, number of teachers employed, and sex-related influences. In classical times the Greek teacher of the young was often a servant or slave, while the major philosophers with great public esteem were teachers of selected adults. The role of priest among early tribes included teaching the rituals to an elite group of young adults, while early childhood education was considered a family affair, and thus had a low social status. Presumably anyone could teach children, but only the wisest could teach adults.

Differences in educational attainment among teachers of various grade levels are obviously related to status in a society which places emphasis on education. The move to require bachelor's degrees for all teachers has tended to balance this aspect of disparity in social status among teachers in elementary and secondary schools. Another factor in internal differences in status is the ratio of male to female teachers in various grade levels. The large proportion of females in elementary teaching, as opposed to the high proportion of males in college teaching, provides status differences as a result of the American cultural view of the female role in society. Occupations in which females have predominated have had difficulty in attaining high social status in America because of sex-role beliefs which view females as subordinate to males. Thus, positions as secretaries, nurses, domestics, and elementary teachers are seen as essentially female jobs and have lower status than positions as doctors, lawyers, engineers, and scientists which are seen as essentially male occupations. This view persists despite increasing numbers of women going into previously male-dominated positions and men going into female-dominated positions.

External Social Role and Status

Role and status are obviously interrelated. Role performance is influenced by the way both the general public and the individual performer perceive the performer's status. John Comenius in 1700 described the teacher's role as follows: "A school is a shop in which young wits are fashioned to virtue, and it is distinguished into forms. The master sitteth in a chair, the scholars in forms; he teacheth, they learn."[1] This is a rather simple explanation of the teacher's role which carries an implicit assumption that the teacher can fashion youngsters to virtue—an apparently worthy social position. George Bernard Shaw's oft-quoted quip that those that can, do, and those that can't, teach, conveys a rather different status element.[2] Jean Rousseau wrote: "There are employments so noble that we cannot fulfill them for money without showing ourselves unworthy to fulfill them. Such an employment is that of a soldier; such a one is that of a teacher."[3]

H. L. Mencken held a contrary view, writing "The average schoolmaster is and always must be essentially an ass, for how can one imagine an intelligent man engaging in so puerile an avocation?"[4] And Mark Twain presented a double-edged comment, "To be good is noble, but to teach others to be good is nobler—and less trouble."[5]

Many scholars have written about what a teacher must have, or be, or do. Each of these sets of requirements for teachers suggests the status of teachers in the eyes of regulation makers. In the early eighteenth century, the Society for the Propagation of the Gospel in Foreign Parts required potential schoolmasters to present certificates attesting to the following particulars: age, marital status, temper, prudence, learning, "sober and pious conversations," zeal in the Christian religion, affection for the present government, and conformity to doctrines and discipline of the Church of England.[6] A contract written in 1682 for a schoolmaster in Flatbush stipulated that he instruct in prayers as well as letters, keep the church clean, ring the bell for services, deliver funeral invitations, dig the grave, "require the students to be friendly in their appearance," and a variety of other tasks.[7]

Rules for teachers posted by the principal of a school in New York City in 1872 required that the teacher bring water and coal for class; that men teachers may take one evening per week for courting (or two evenings if they attended church regularly); that women teachers who get married or "engage in unseemly conduct" will be fired; and that any teacher who smokes, drinks, frequents pool or public halls, or gets shaved in a barber shop will be under suspicion for lack of integrity, worth, and honesty.[8] A teacher's contract in North Carolina in the 1930s carried these admonitions: a promise to abstain from all dancing and immodest dress, not to go out with young men except as it is necessary to stimulate Sunday school work, not to fall in love, and to remain on the school grounds when not actively engaged in school or church work.[9]

Until recent times teachers were not permitted to smoke on school property, and in many schools teachers are still limited to smoking in prescribed areas away from students. In some districts and states teachers face numerous restrictions on determination of course content, what teaching materials can be used, and some forms of personal behavior. Some schools have dress regulations for teachers, time clocks for punching in and out of work, requirements that letters from teachers to parents pass through an administrator's office for clearance, admonitions to teachers about political activities outside of school, and related concerns. Many states have specific regulations covering the teacher's use of materials and curriculum.[10] One district board of education passed a regulation that any materials which dealt with Russia had to be approved by the board before they could be used in classes.[11]

These restrictions are indicative of the social status and perception of role accorded to teachers by society. There seems to be a culturally derived fear of education in America, accompanied by a strong belief in the value of schooling, that creates one of a number of role conflicts for teachers. Transmission of the cultural heritage to younger generations, so long as it does not challenge the commonly held social values, is the primary role expected of teachers. Constraints on teachers occur most often in areas where the potential of critical examination of social ideas is most evident, for example, in English and social studies. This happens mainly in schools below the college level, and is related to the anti-intellectualism described by Hofstadter.[12] Zeigler cites many illustrations of the fears inherent in classroom teaching.[13]

Role expectations of teachers by parents constitute another influence on role performance, and these expectations also reflect status. School situations vary in the amount of contact between parents and teachers (elementary schools generally have more contact), but pressure from parents occurs directly through person-to-person dialogues, institutionally through parent organizations like the PTA, and indirectly through public relations concerns of school boards and administrators. In addition, the teacher knows that parents will be judging the results of the teachers' efforts through their children's behavior. Although a professional status is assumed by teachers, the role expectation of parents is likely to be more that of a service occupation. Goslin suggests that teachers are a marginally professional group, as indicated by answers to the question, "To whom does the child belong?" given by lawyers, doctors, and teachers in their roles as advisors.[14] Goslin points out that attempts of parents to influence the teaching process are related to variables such as "the relative social class backgrounds of the teacher and the family, the extent to which the community in general takes an active interest in the school, and the degree to which the subject matter is of a highly specialized nature."[15]

Social Class and the Teacher

As illustrated earlier, dimensions of social class are related to education in a variety of ways. In this section the social-class backgrounds of teachers are examined. Presumably the social-class origins of a teacher will influence his perceptions of role expectations in his job in such ways as status relations to parents, students, and peers; class-held values; and normative behavior patterns. The origins of teachers in relation to their achieved social status is also a measure of mobility. If teachers come from lower-social-class families and teaching is a higher social-status position, then upward mobility is an important motivation for entry into the field. If the reverse is true, then downward mobility is a consideration to potential entrants.

Studies of social-class origins of teachers indicate that prior to the 1920s, teachers were generally recruited from the middle class. Urbanization, compulsory education and increased emphasis on higher levels of schooling led to the recruitment of larger numbers of teachers, and the teaching field became more heterogeneous in social-class makeup. Although the majority of teachers still come from middle-class homes, there is greater representation from working-class origins in teaching now. Elsbree, indicated in 1939 that teachers were predominantly of lower-middle-class origin.[16] Havighurst and Neugarten report a series of studies made between 1940 and 1950 which also concluded that the majority of teachers came from lower-middle class families. A national sample of teachers in 1960–1961, as reported by Havighurst and Neugarten, showed occupation of the teacher's father to be distributed as follows: farmer, 26.5 percent; skilled or semiskilled worker, 23.4 percent; managerial, 22 percent; professional, 14.5 percent; clerical or sales, 7.1 percent; and unskilled worker, 6.5 percent. These data also show that 40 percent of the oldest teachers (over age 56) had fathers who were farmers, while only 20 percent of the youngest (under 26) were from farm backgrounds; and that only 1.9 percent of the oldest group had fathers who were unskilled workers, while 7.6 percent of the youngest were in that category.[17]

Richard Carlson, in a study conducted in California, found that socioeconomic variance in the origins of teachers was related to grade level taught and sex. His data show that "teachers have origins at all levels of the social class continuum."[18] But 4.4 percent of the female elementary teachers were from upper-class origins, while 1.1 percent of the male secondary teachers were of that class. Almost 30 percent of the sample of female elementary teachers were from the upper two classes, compared to 7 percent of the male secondary teachers. Male secondary teachers from upper-lower-class origins accounted for over 40 percent of the sample; only about 20 percent of the female elementary teachers were from that class.

Social class studies tend to agree on the proportions of population in each social class. In comparison with this presumed distribution of the total population into various social classes, Carlson's data revealed that teachers in the sample came from the upper three classes in far larger proportions than did the total population, and were underrepresentative of the lower classes. That is, a larger percentage of teachers came from families classified as upper-upper than is true of the total population. Teachers were not drawn from the lower-lower class in any proportion near to the distribution of that class in society.[19]

Social mobility of teachers is another area of interest to sociologists of education. Joel Gerstl notes that three-fifths of beginning teachers have moved above the occupational status of their fathers.[20] He cites a number of studies to indicate that teaching represents upward mobility for many people, especially for males.[21] McGuire and White suggested that the frequency of upward mobility among the Texas teachers analyzed was above 40 percent.[22] Carlson determined that female elementary teachers do not seem to evince upward social mobility as a group, but male secondary teachers show considerable upward mobility.[23]

It is difficult to judge how much influence social-class origins and mobility exert on the role performance of teachers. Conclusive data are not available. We can hypothesize, however, that the higher social-class female entrants perceive teaching as a social service, while the male entrants view it as a means of upward mobility. The effect on education of both viewpoints is a continuance of conformist patterns to a middle-class morality. The female teachers, drawn from classes which value the *status quo*, are not likely to make drastic alterations; and male teachers, who desire the mobility afforded by teaching, will not react against the system they anticipate joining. Dramatic breakthroughs in education, be they scientific or humanistic, are not likely to occur under such circumstances.

Internal Role Expectations

Within the school, teachers perform a number of roles depending upon expectations of the referent group with which they are confronted.

TEACHER-PUPIL ROLES

Willard Waller, in a classic analysis of teaching published in 1932, noted the dominance-submission relationship between teacher and student and the authority role virtually demanded of the teacher. He states that "Friendly attitudes must spring up only in a situation defined in terms of teacher domination."[24] Brookover supplements this role expectation by coupling it to the effectiveness of teachers in the classroom, suggesting that a lack of dominance behavior by teachers is likely to result in a loss in teaching effectiveness.[25] The antagonistic relationship between teachers and pupils in which the teacher, as a result of frustrations in role expectations and performance, acts against the best interests of students is portrayed by Edgar Friedenberg.[26] He indicates that the teacher of bright students often suffers from *ressentiment*, a "kind of free-floating ill-temper" that results from frustrations in achieving expectation in a socially mobile society.

TEACHER-ADMINISTRATOR ROLES

Waller describes the differences in communication among roles in the schools and notes that the teacher speaking to an administrator is deferential, while in speaking to a student he is authoritarian.[27] This conveys the nature of role expectation and performance that exists between teachers and their administrators. The general relationship is that of employer-employee, rather than that of colleagues. In the public schools both administrators and teachers are employees of the public, and the school board serves as employer. The management-labor dichotomy which affects civil service and other public employment is also demonstrated in the schools and often becomes as diverse in interest and perspective there as in the private sector. The developing militancy of teacher associations and the withdrawal of administration personnel from them indicates this disparity in viewpoint. The battle over organization of teachers between the American Federation of Teachers (an affiliate of the AFL-CIO) and the National Education Association has widened this gap. Emphasis on scientific management training for school administrators, now a prominent trend in the field, may increase the difference in viewpoint even further. There is an obvious interrelationship among teachers and administrators, but suspicion, alienation, and differing viewpoints pose role expectations and performances which separate the two groups.

Another aspect of this relationship is the widely held view that professional advancement means moving from teaching into administration. This mobility factor serves to maintain a dominance-submission role difference, since the teacher who desires to move upward must adopt a nonthreatening role in relation to the administrator. Friedenberg suggests that "The life style of the public high school teacher remains, characteristically, that of the dutiful subordinate awaiting preferment in a niggardly bureaucratic structure."[28]

TEACHER-TEACHER ROLES

Teachers' role expectations vary. There are different norms of behavior and expectations among teachers of differing grade levels. As with most peer groups, teachers who veer widely from the norms are suspect and are treated with aloofness, disdain, ostracism, or other forms of social punishment by their fellow teachers. Conformity in matters of dress, speech, and manner are common, especially in the lower school levels. Elementary teachers tend to view themselves as models for behavior of their students. Secondary teachers share this to some extent, but college teachers have considerably less concern for model behavior in personal and social areas. The likelihood of an unshaven, tieless, relatively disheveled male teacher is less in elementary schools than in colleges. This is partly because of external pressures from parents and school boards, and partly because of peer pressure. One of the first things a student teacher learns in local schools is to change his dress and manner from the relatively free and casual style of students to the more restrained and formal style of teachers. This socialization occurs mainly through peer influence.

Professional role expectations among teachers include such behaviors as apportioning equitable homework assignments, carrying papers, attending committee meetings, being punctual in meeting a class, joining or not joining a teacher organization, maintaining a level of secrecy about teaching practices, and being aware of specific local issues. Teachers tend to be very sensitive to one-upmanship practices by other teachers, and this results in a system of rewards for seniority, socially enforced levels of modesty about quality of teaching or innovations, and peer skepticism toward new teachers and others who have not been long-term associates. This is, of course, no different from peer pressures in most groups.

Role Conflicts in Teaching

Teaching is an amorphous and ambiguous field. It encompasses nursery school training, football coaching, graduate tutorials in nuclear physics, lectures to hundreds of students on Western civilization, field trips to a farm, watching a movie on Brazil, plugging a student into a computer, and listening to speeches. Its ambiguity comes from the variety of roles expected and played for varying groups in differing situations and for diverse purposes.

Conflicts in roles of teachers occur in several instances. Havighurst and Neugarten suggest a number of roles of teachers. Included are the teacher's roles as: (1) mediator of learning, (2) disciplinarian, (3) judge, (4) confidante, (5) surrogate of middle-class morality, (6) participant in community affairs, (7) sociological stranger, and (8) social reformer.[29]

There are evident conflicts among these roles, such as the conflict between sociological stranger and participant in community affairs. The teacher who is expected to be involved in activities like fund drives and church dinners is often alienated from the community, which may view him as some sort of ideal type of strange apparition.

Another obvious role conflict is that between the desire for social reform through education and the conservative nature of prevalent middle-class ideas. The teacher is presumed to be a conservative force in maintaining the moral standards acceptable to the middle class but is also supposed to improve society by working with the young. The reformer may be in direct conflict with the established norms which he is presumed to be teaching. This conflict is a very difficult one for a teacher who realizes a need to improve society but has middle-class inclinations by virtue of his origins or his strivings for upward mobility.

As transmitter of learning, the teacher is expected to be an expert but still to be a public servant. This conflict is evident when parents visit the school and talk to teachers as public servants even while demanding that they teach sophisticated material. It is also indicated by the fact that state legislatures, boards of education, and administrators choose much of the material to be taught without permitting the teacher to enter into the decision. The expertise expected of teachers often is not relied upon by administrators or boards for some curricular decisions.

Within the school the roles of disciplinarian, judge, and confidante of students are in obvious conflict. The teacher must punish for misdeeds, judge academic performance with grades, and still strive to gain rapport with each pupil. His role as parental substitute, with its consequent conflicts, is unlike that of many other professions. The lawyer, doctor, architect, and engineer generally do not accept such roles, although psychologists, depending upon their training and interest, often do. In the teacher's case, however, the role is expected by the parent and the school system, and the child is compelled by law to attend. The parent tacitly agrees to the teacher's role as his substitute, but may be suspicious of the teacher in his performance of that role.

Jacques Barzun, in his eloquent *Teacher in America*, writes of these conflicts in terms of the teacher's value.

Then begins the fierce, secret struggle out of which education may come—the struggle between home and school, parent and child child and teacher; the struggle also that lies deep within the parent and within society concerning the teacher's worth: Is this man of knowledge to be looked up to as wise and helpful, or to be looked down on as at once servile and dangerous, capable and inglorious, higher than the parent yet lower than the brat?[30]

Summary

Teachers are at once influential and servile, scholars and chumps, leaders and followers, anxious and secure. The roles played by teachers are various and often conflicting. The status ascribed to them is both high and low. Teachers are subject to stereotype, yet each has individual characteristics. These social dimensions show the dynamic nature of the occupation and the resulting difficulty in making generalizations about it. Observations of the behavior of teachers from the perspective of the institutional models provided in earlier chapters provides an approach to analyzing teacher status, role, and role conflict.

NOTES

1. John Amos Comenius, *Orbis Sennalium Pictus*, 1700, as found in Marjorie Smiley and John Diekhoff, *Prologue to Teaching*, Oxford University Press, Fair Lawn, N.J., 1959, inside cover.
2. George Bernard Shaw, *Maxims for Revolutionists*, found in Burton Stevenson, *The Home Book of Quotations*, Dodd, Mead & Co., New York, 1967, p. 1971.
3. From Smiley and Diekhoff, p. 29.
4. H. L. Mencken, *Prejudices*, found in Stevenson, *op. cit.*, p. 1971.
5. From Rudolph Flesch, *The New Book of Unusual Quotations*, Harper & Row, New York, 1966, p. 380.
6. From Smiley and Diekhoff, p. 20.
7. Daniel J. Pratt, *Annals of Public Education in the State of New*

York from 1626 to 1746, The Argus Co., Albany, 1872, pp. 65–67.
8. From Dorothy Westby-Gibson, *Social Perspectives on Education*, John Wiley & Sons, New York, 1965, p. 425.
9. From Smiley and Diekhoff, *Prologue to Teaching*, p. 32.
10. Jack L. Nelson, "Nationalism and Education," *Buffalo Studies*, vol. 3, no. 3, 1967, pp. 113–132.
11. Personal experience of the author and interviews with participants.
12. Richard Hofstadter, *Anti-Intellectualism in American Life*, Knopf, New York, 1963.
13. Harmon Zeigler, *The Political Life of American Teachers*, Prentice-Hall, Englewood Cliffs, N.J., 1967, chaps. 4, 5. See also, Jack Nelson and Gene Roberts, *The Censors and The Schools*, Little, Brown, Boston, 1963.
14. David A. Goslin, *The School in Contemporary Society*, Scott, Foresman, Chicago, 1965, p. 35.
15. *Ibid.*
16. Willard S. Elsbree, *The American Teacher*, American Book, New York, 1939, p. 410.
17. National Education Association, *The American Public School Teacher, 1960–1961*, NEA, Washington, D.C., 1963, as adapted and reported in Robert J. Havighurst and Bernice L. Neugarten, *Society and Education*, Allyn and Bacon, Boston, p. 410-H.
18. Richard O. Carlson, "Variation and Myth in the Social Status of Teachers," *The Journal of Educational Sociology*, November, 1951, p. 117.
19. *Ibid.*, pp. 104–118.
20. Joel E. Gerstl, "Education and the Sociology of Work," found in Hansen and Gerstl, *On Education–Sociological Perspectives*, p. 236. John Wiley and Sons, New York, 1967.
21. *Ibid.*, with reference to Ward S. Mason, *The Beginning Teacher: Status and Career Orientations*, U.S. Department of Health, Education and Welfare, Office of Education, Government Printing Office, Washington, D.C., 1961; James A. Davis, *Great Aspirations*, Aldine, Chicago, 1964; and John L. Colombotos, *Sources of Professionalism: A Study of High School Teachers*, U.S. Office of Education, Government Printing Office, Washington, D.C., 1962.
22. Carson McGuire, and George D. White, "Social Origins of Teachers—Some Facts from the Southwest," found in Lindley J. Stiles, *The Teacher's Role in American Society*, Fourteenth Yearbook of the John Dewey Society, New York, 1957.
23. Carlson, p. 117.
24. Willard Waller, *The Sociology of Teaching*, Wiley, New York, 1932.
25. Wilbur B. Brookover, "Social Roles of Teachers and Pupil Achievements," *American Sociological Review*, 1943, pp. 389–393.
26. Edgar Z. Friedenberg, "The Gifted Student and His Enemies," *Commentary*, May, 1962, as found in Linton and Nelson, *Patterns of Power*, pp. 534–545.
27. Waller, *op. cit.*
28. Friedenberg, *op. cit.*, p. 537.
29. Havighurst and Neugarten, *op. cit.*, pp. 431–453.
30. Jacques Barzun, *Teacher in America*, Anchor Books, Doubleday, Garden City, N.Y., 1954, p. 11.

PART IV

ATYPICAL BEHAVIOR

The preceding chapters have attempted to define, describe, and analyze schools in several dimensions. They have relied upon normal data, typical behaviors in usual situations, and generalizing theory. Abnormal data, atypical behaviors, and exceptions to generalizations have been considered only briefly and not systematically. Because individuals vary and institutional responses differ in time and space, it would be impossible to deal comprehensively with the myriad deviations possible in social and school behaviors of individuals. Part IV presents some of the most clear examples of deviance and institutional response as illustrative of this area of sociology of education.

Chapter 13 / *Student Careers*

Part II provided general models for analyzing the school. The primary focus of these models was on institutional structure, patterns of leadership, spheres of influence, and inherited culture; they did not deal extensively with the individual in the institution. This chapter therefore presents a model for analyzing the way in which institutions deal with individuals. The chapters which follow are primarily examples of some of the major areas of conflict within the school and of the way in which the school deals with atypical students: juvenile delinquents (Chapter 14) and mentally disturbed students (Chapter 15).

The Designation of Roles

In order to function efficiently and with the least amount of conflict, institutions attempt to place actors in roles which are mutually acceptable to the institution and to the individual. The ideal actor, of course, is the one who accepts the definition presented to him by the institution either because he agreed with it before he entered or because he is willing to accept any role which an institution gives him. With such a person there is little conflict between the institution and the individual; the individual feels fulfilled in that he can do what he feels he needs to do, and the institution is satisfied in that the required work is performed.

Should the individual actor have a totally different set of norms, it is still possible for the institution to mold him so that he will be willing to accept the role presented to him. An extreme example of an institution successfully changing the self-concept of an individual for its own purposes is the Communist Chinese method of dealing with American prisoners during the Korean War. As Eugene Kindead reports,[1] the Communists did not attempt to maintain escape-proof facilities; rather, they worked from the premise that escape involves cooperation between inmates and, therefore, if they could eliminate cooperation they could also eliminate the possibility of escape. Through various group techniques the Communists were able to convince the inmates that informing on one another was not only acceptable but also praiseworthy. Special gifts and prizes were awarded to men who informed about even the most insignificant behaviors such as stealing an extra bowl of soup or not making a bed correctly. As opposed to World War II, where Americans were noted for their ability to cooperate and organize escapes, during the Korean War Americans were noted for their inability to cooperate or organize. What the Communists had done, in effect, was to change the career pattern of the inmates from one of cooperation and organization to one of distrust, malice, and informing.

It should not be assumed that all institutional change is detrimental. Under normal circumstances change may be of mutual benefit to the institution and to the individual. For example, it is necessary for the family and the school to act as primary agents in remolding the child from a purely egotistical being to a more altruistic being. This change, which is usually accomplished over a long period of time and in a relatively gentle fashion, is imperative to the individual and the institution as well as to society in general.

Whether the change is gentle or sudden, helpful or detrimental, how does the institution exact it? This chapter attempts to answer this question.

Transience or Permanence of Role

The process of accepting the societal definition of the self has been discussed by various writers, but none has discussed it more systematically than Thomas J. Scheff.[2] Scheff attempts to determine the societal pressures which cause transitory eccentricities to become permanent deviant behaviors.

Though Scheff does not discuss it, it is possible by inference to deduce that the patterns which cause transitory deviance to become career deviance are the same as those which would cause transitory positive behaviors to become permanent positive behaviors (such as becoming a "good student" or a "good citizen"). By implication it can be used to discuss any form of career behavior of an individual within an institution.

Specifically, Scheff asks three questions:

1. Under what conditions do various forms of deviant behavior become stable and uniform?
2. To what extent are symptoms of deviant behavior the result of conforming to societal definitions of stereotypic behavior?
3. Are there certain contingencies which lead to the definition of deviant behavior?

Scheff begins his discussion by distinguishing between residual and nonresidual deviance. *Nonresidual deviance* refers to recognized categories of deviant behavior with specific traits, while *residual deviance* includes all the forms of deviant behavior for which there is no specific category. For example, the catatonic schizophrenic has certain psychotic behavioral patterns which distinguish him from other deviants, while "mental illness" may include everything from psychosomatic disorders to nervous breakdowns. Schizophrenia is a nonresidual category, while mental illness is a residual category. Scheff is interested in residual deviance, that is, those disorders which will be defined differently by different people (including experts) and which will affect behavior by the way in which they are defined.

For example, if a cold is defined as hay fever, the sufferer continues his daily pattern of existence. If, however, the cold is defined as potential pneumonia, the patient is put to bed (This relates to question 1, above). Also, to what extent will the definition of hay fever or pneumonia cause the sufferer to pattern his behavior after what he thinks should be the symptoms of his disease. Will he act differently if he thinks he has no fever versus a high fever, if he should be just "not feeling well" as opposed to needing "complete bed-rest" (this relates to question 2 above).

Once Scheff has made the distinction between residual and nonresidual deviance, he focuses his attention on the way in which primary (transitory) deviance becomes a secondary or permanent career pattern for an actor. He postulates that the major factors influencing the career patterns of an actor are the definitions placed upon that actor and upon his role by the institution (this relates to question 3).

Labeling

In the case of mental illness, Scheff indicates that the most common societal reaction is one of denial; that is, the society would rather label behavior "eccentric" than "mentally ill." According to Scheff, as long as the person is labeled as an eccentric or as "going through a phase" the chances are that the residual deviance will be transitory since the deviant behavior will not have been reinforced. On the other hand, if the behavior is reinforced there is a greater likelihood that it will become fixed and that the deviance will become permanent.

This might explain Hollingshead and Redlich's finding that the lower class has fewer neurotics than the middle and upper classes.[3] Since Scheff would define neurosis as a residual deviance (it is largely an undefined category), the most important factor determining the permanence of the neurosis should be whether or not it is reinforced. Hollingshead and Redlich's study indicates that members of the lower class who show neurotic tendencies do not have the money to obtain psychological help and they have to learn to live with their unreinforced neuroses. For this reason, according to Scheff's hypothesis, lower-class neurosis would tend to be transitory while middle- and upper-class neurotics, who have the money to obtain help, would be reinforced in their neuroses and thereby would become career neurotics.

Scheff presents nine propositions to show the effect of labeling upon the definition of deviance:

1. Residual deviance has varied sources.
2. The rate of unrecorded residual deviance is extremely high.
3. Most residual deviance is denied and is transitory.
4. The imagery of stereotypes of deviance are learned in early childhood.
5. The stereotypes or deviance are reaffirmed, inadvertently, in daily interaction.
6. Once the society has labeled the deviant, he is rewarded for playing the deviant role.
7. The deviant is negatively sanctioned for attempting to leave the role.
8. When the institution attempts to label the individual, he may feel that no other opinion is open to him except the institutional definition.
9. In residual deviance, labeling is the single most important factor contributing to career deviance.

In relation to proposition 1, for example, it has been shown that mental illness can be caused by genetic, physiological, and nutritional as well as traditional psychological sources. Career patterns of students within the school also originate from diverse sources. The home situation, the absence or presence of one or both parents, the attitudes and teachings of previous teachers, and the area of the country where the child was reared could all be listed as contributing to the career pattern of the student.

Scheff's second proposition, that there is a high rate of unrecognized residual deviance, is of less concern here except to note its validity and to indicate the tendency on the part of an institution to ignore deviant behavior. For example, if the preconception of the school is such that it believes that boys tend to get into innocent mischief, there is a greater likelihood that behavior which could predict juvenile delinquency would be denied or brushed aside with the admonition that "boys will be boys." If, on the other hand, the preconception is such that misbehavior is defined as delinquency, there is greater likelihood that innocent mischief will be denied in favor of defining the behavior as deviant. In either case, the determining factor is not the behavior itself but the desire of the institution to ignore behavioral implications which are contrary to the accepted definition.

The third proposition, that there is a relationship between denial of the symptoms and the ephemerality of the disorder, is central to Scheff's thesis. In effect, if you don't mention the disorder, it will go away. Indeed in the case of stutterers, if the infirmity is not mentioned and if nothing is done, the stuttering often will pass. If the parents become concerned and make a fuss over the stuttering, however, there is some reason to believe that it will continue. Scheff points out that a number of forms of deviant behavior occur in children, such as temper tantrums, biting, thumb sucking, or imagining nonexistent playmates or ghosts. Yet these behaviors are normally transitory. Adults, too, engage in transitory deviant behavior; they may talk to themselves, daydream, or steal from libraries, but unless the behavior is reinforced, it does not become a career pattern.

A particularly striking instance which bears out Scheff's proposition that any form of deviant behavior will tend to be transitory if the behavior is not reinforced is Eysenck's study[4] of a large number of diagnosed schizophrenics, only half of whom could be treated immediately. The others were required to go through their normal daily activities for a period of up to a year. At the end of that year, much to everyone's surprise, those who had not been treated for schizophrenia were in no worse condition than those who had been treated. According to Scheff's proposition, the ones who were being treated for schizophrenia had been reinforced in deviance by being treated, whereas those who were not being treated did not have their behavior reinforced; they had to learn to live with it, and their deviance not only did not increase, but they actually adapted to the new situation with some facility.

Again the basic question is raised as to the difference between factors which allow deviance to remain transitory and the factors which seem to make deviance permanent. Scheff postulates that the primary factor involved is social reaction to the behavior. He discusses Glass's experiments with battle fatigue in Korea[5] to illustrate his point. Glass discovered that when men who sincerely thought they were suffering from battle fatigue were told that their symptoms were nothing unusual and certainly nothing to worry about, the rate of withdrawal from the front lines dropped appreciably. The theory is that since the symptoms were denied, the "mental disorder" disappeared. To hypothesize a more familiar situation, what would be the effect of reinforcing success on students who had a history of failure in classes? Is there a possible relationship between being failed in a class and considering oneself an academic failure?

Scheff's fourth proposition is that the imagery of mental disorder (or mental and social health and stability) is learned in early childhood. Through the mass media, remarks of adults, bizarre farces of the insane, and so forth, the child picks up a series of cues which form the basis for a definition of mental deviance. For our purposes, it seems plausible to assume that the same communication forces present cues to the child which define the school and student in that school as well as teachers and administrators. Judging by the studies of the public's stereotyped role expectations for teachers, it would seem that the process of presenting cues about the school to children might be more advanced than the cues about mental disorders; that is, the imagery of the school is also learned and firmly imprinted from early childhood.

Scheff's fifth proposition indicates that stereotypes are reaffirmed in daily life; even though adults gain a great deal of information relating to mental disorders (and by extension, to the school) the original stereotypes remain alongside the new information. There seem to be two reasons for this: the earlier cues are firmly imprinted, and the mass media continue the stereotype. For example, if the school's stereotype of lower-class students is that they are not capable of learning, the school will tend to deny data which runs counter to the stereotype.

It is quite certain that the school has preconceived notions about the abilities of various types of students and these stereotypes are reconfirmed by mass media, informal communication with other teachers, and so forth. In terms of achievement, teachers tend to equate family background and socioeconomic status with academic ability, even though the Lynds in *Middletown*[6] and Riessman in *The Culturally Deprived Child*[7] have shown the equation to be fallacious. The researchers indicate that the lower-class child has a greater interest in learning and that his parents, though they may be uneducated themselves, share this faith in education. Nevertheless, the stereotype is so entrenched that the data are denied, and the school continues to operate on the assumption that the lower-class child has neither the ability nor the desire to learn.

Scheff's sixth and seventh propositions indicate that once the society has labeled the individual a deviant he is rewarded for playing the deviant role and negatively sanctioned for not playing it. For instance, if teachers expect poorer performance from the lower-class students, they will have a tendency to lower the academic expectations of these students. If the teacher assumes that the lower-class black student in a remedial class is incapable of writing an essay, he will not be required to write one. Since most students are pleased to get out of work, the lower-class black remedial student is reinforced in his role of the poor student. On the other hand, a new teacher who does not feel that these students are incapable may blithely assign essays every week and receive them every week. The more common school practice positively reinforces the residual deviant role of the poor student.

With regard to negative sanctions for attempting to leave the deviant role, let us further speculate that a teacher believes students are not capable of writing essays, but one student denies the role and turns in a well-written one. If the teacher's preconception is sufficiently strong, he will assume another explanation—perhaps that the student had someone else write it for him or that he copied it out of a book. The teacher may believe that he is punishing the student for cheating when in actuality the student is punished for leaving the deviant role.

Once the deviant feels that other avenues have been closed, he may consider that the only option open is to accept the deviant role. In the example used, the student may come to accept the school's definition of himself as a poor student. This is Scheff's eighth proposition: the individual has attempted to maintain the conventional role, has failed, and has been negatively sanctioned for trying to leave the deviant role; he thus assumes that deviance is the only option left to him.

Up to this point, we have been stressing society's attempt to label the individual. Most of this labeling is external to the individual's self-concept; that is, the individual's definition may still be quite different from that presented to him by the institution. If the labeling practices of the institution are sufficiently effective, however, the individual will eventually incorporate the institution's definition into his own self-concept and become a career deviant. For example, when the school's definition of the poor student is reinforced a sufficient number of times through successive failures, he comes to think of himself as a failure. His primary deviance becomes career deviance.

Scheff's last proposition and his major conclusion is that labeling, rather than any actual offense or behavior, is the single most important factor in the establishment of career deviance. The extent and direction (positive or negative) of labeling is determined largely by the societal reaction to specific behaviors. Part of this reaction is determined by the history of interaction between the individual and the institution and the preconceptions and points of view based on that history. The severity of negative reaction, however, is also based on three factors inherent in the specific situation. The three factors listed by Scheff bear a striking similarity to a Marxian analysis:

The first factor is the visibility, amount, and degree of deviance; that is, how overt is the behavior of the deviant individual? The definition of the visibility of course, depends largely on the institution. For example, being three minutes late to a social engagement is certainly an acceptable length of time. On the other hand, being three minutes late to a junior high school class is not acceptable. When a student walks in three minutes late, he is highly visible in that everyone in the classroom is fully aware that he is late. Another example would be heterosexual relations which would be perfectly acceptable in dating or in marriage but would be unacceptable, and quite visible, in the school.

The second factor is the power of the individual deviant and the distance between him and the agent of social control. The more powerful or the more distant the deviant, the less will be the effect of the labeling. For example, if the deviant student's father is a member of the school board, the deviance may be ignored or glossed over rather than systematically punished. In this case the individual may have powers which are greater than some of the teachers or administrators in the school.

The third factor is the tolerance level and preconceptions of the institution. The tolerance level determines to a large extent the behaviors which will be considered deviant. Of course, it is also defined in terms of particular institutional situations and the situation of the individual within the institution. For example, throwing rocks at trees or old houses is considered reasonably acceptable behavior in the country; however, such behavior is not acceptable in any form in a populated area such as a city.

In all these categories, certain students are more prone to the labeling process than are others. The lower-class minority-group child is often more visible in terms of color, speech habits, and poorer dress. He, his family, and his particular community have the least amount of power of any group in the society. Furthermore, because he is a child in an adult-run institution, his power is again decreased when his distance from the authorities (teachers, administrators, and counselors) is diminished. Because of the preconceptions of the school, the tolerance level may be lowered so that deviant behavior which is sometimes called "good clean fun" in other schools or at other times now becomes malicious mischief. All this indicates that the power of the school to label individuals and the individual's acceptance of the label will be different with different types of students. Nevertheless, the basic hypothesis that the school is a potential labeler and the labels can effectively change the behavior of at least certain of the students still holds.

Summary

This chapter has presented an analytical model of labeling in the school. No value bias is intended, since the school's role as labeler can have a positive as well as a negative effect upon students. Negative effects tend to be more graphic, however, and are therefore used as a heuristic device. It is true, however, that much of the school's labeling is negative in nature; there are less honor students and they are less effectively labeled than "bad boys" and "bad girls."

Regardless of the specific outcome, the school can and does label and can obtain acquiescence to its labels from its students. The labeling process is a primary source of the school's power as an institution. Once the school can get the student to accept its definition of his role, then it will be in a position of great power over the student.

In the two following chapters, specific instances in which the school has successfully labeled students will be discussed. The chapters describe extreme situations—juvenile delinquency and mental disturbance—but the process by which the school labels is the same regardless of the severity of the deviance. Only the severity of the reaction changes.

NOTES

1. Eugene Kindead, *In Every War But One*, Norton, New York, 1959.
2. Thomas J. Scheff, "The Role of the Mentally Ill and the Dynamics of Mental Disorder: A Research Framework," *Sociometry*, 1963, vol. 26, no. 4, pp. 436–453.
3. August Hollingshead and Frederick C. Redlich, *Social Class and Mental Illness*, Wiley, New York, 1958.
4. H. J. Eysenck, "The Effects of Psychotherapy: An Evaluation," *Journal of Consulting Psychology*, vol. 16, 1952, pp. 319–324.
5. L. J. Glass, "Psychotherapy in the Combat Zone," Symposium on Stress, Army Medical Service Graduate School, Washington, D.C., 1953.
6. Robert S. Lynd and Hellen Merrell Lynd, *Middletown*, Harvest Books, Harcourt, Brace & World, New York, 1956.
7. Frank Riessman, *The Culturally Deprived Child*, Harper & Row, New York, 1962.

Chapter 14 / *The School and the Juvenile Delinquent*

This chapter attempts to formulate a theory of the school's role in juvenile delinquency. Many writers have indicated that the school is a major factor in the lives of juvenile delinquents but none has discussed the operational parameters of this role systematically.

Theoretical Formulation

David Matza, in his *Delinquency and Drift*,[1] presents the following theory of how a person becomes delinquent:

1. All people have contact with and take their orientation from the predominant culture (in our case, middle-class culture). This is not to say that all people are the same, but rather, as Cohen has pointed out,[2] that everyone desires these values.

This chapter first appeared as "Deviant Student Behavior and the Role of the School" in *Urban Education*, vol. 2, no. 1, winter, 1965, pp. 27–34.

2. Through various processes (such as a sense of injustice) neutralization takes place, and the values of the dominant culture are superseded.
3. This causes an anomic state which Matza calls *drift*.
4. Drift is not a sufficient cause for delinquency, but it is a necessary one.
5. Preparation (learning through experience that one can violate the prescribed rules) and desperation ("the mood of fatalism [which] . . . refers to the experience of seeing one's self as effect"), predispose the juvenile to the delinquent act. Delinquency is not a necessary consequence of preparation and desperation, but preparation and desperation are necessary antecedents.

The School and the Deviant Student: The Institution's Point of View

As discussed previously, the school has a predominantly middle-class orientation. According to Carlson,[3] while teachers may at one time have had a uniform middle-class origin, they no longer do. Carlson does not mention, however, that, regardless of the class origin of the teacher, his orientation would normally be considered middle-class. For instance, Doyle[4] notes that the teacher's own internalized beliefs about appropriate classroom behavior are noticeably affected by interaction with his direct supervisor, who, having been chosen by the predominantly middle-class institution, manifests a middle-class attitude. As Brookover has pointed out, "The concern for property, proper sex conduct, good manners, neatness and cleanliness, as well as initiative, self-reliance and individual responsibility for one's behavior, are emphasized as basic characteristics in the image of the good school citizen."[5] He further states that "children are also expected to behave in accordance with the moral code and manners prevailing in the dominant groups. If this behavior has not been previously acquired, teachers generally expect students to learn it in school."

The school defines deviances, specifically juvenile delinquency, in terms of infractions.[6] The question then becomes, "What does the school define as an *infraction*?" Or, to put it another way, "How does one come to be labeled as a 'bad boy'?"

Henry[7] points out that girls in general are subject only to the infraction regarding heterosexual sex play, whereas boys are subject to a whole host of infractions. According to Henry, the reason for this is that the rules of the school are very similar to the values which girls are expected to maintain *outside the school.* As an example of this, it has been pointed out that most of the infractions which teachers consider serious are of an overt, active nature. More important, they are of a nature whereby the *infractions within the school are similar to the values held outside of the school* by most males: laughing, talking, wise-cracking, bossing or dominating others, ridiculing, and making noise. The boy is at a disadvantage in the school, since behavior which is expected of him outside is considered an infraction inside.

Furthermore, if one assumes that the lower-class boy will be more prone to such things as "sounding," and noisiness in his behavior outside the school, then it should be even more difficult for him to follow the feminine, middle-class value system imposed upon him in the school.

Infractions within the school are usually punished. Counselors have neither the time nor the interest to deal with individual behavior problems. An assistant principal is often in charge of disciplinary problems. His solutions may involve many variables (family background of the student, athletic status of the student, number of previous offenses, and so forth, but the usual punishment involves staying after school, social adjustment class (the back ward), unsatisfactory citizenship grades, suspension, or expulsion (he can usually only recommend this, but his recommendations are often followed). All these measures are punitive, yet, as Schanley[8] has pointed out, punitive measures are dysfunctional in that they only extend the frustration-aggression syndrome.

At this point, we will not discuss whether or not the definition of infraction which is used by the school is a valid one. It is sufficient that the definition is designed in a middle-class, feminine, withdrawn mode, and that the definition effects the process of labeling.

Labeling

The problem of labeling in mental illness has an interesting counterpart in the labeling of "bad boys" in the school. As discussed in Chapter 13, Scheff[9] postulates that there are two types of deviance: nonresidual (those for which there are definite categories such as schizophrenia or car theft) and residual ("waste basket" categories which include all deviance for which we have only vague, nonspecific labels such as *mental illness* or *bad boy*). Scheff's article deals almost exclusively with the residual category. His basic thesis is that the process of labeling can be as much the cause of the residual deviance as the deviance itself. Scheff's hypothesis can be viewed as a special case of Merton's "self-fulfilling prophecy." He suggests that the deviant passes through stages. In the primary stage the deviant exhibits eccentricities but has not been labeled as a deviant by the society. The primary deviant is, to a large extent, an occasional deviant. Once a label has been attached to a primary deviant, however, the stage of secondary deviance has begun. The first part of the process is external labeling by the society, which thereby places the student in a residual deviant category. At this stage, the deviant may or may not believe himself to be justifiably in the deviant category. Once the deviant accepts the label, however, he is a full-fledged secondary deviant and in many ways a career deviant. Furthermore, even when he is not a career deviant and wants to leave the deviant category (which would be unlikely, since he often believes the label himself), society makes it very difficult for him to do so. He finds that society expects him to play the deviant role and places negative sanctions on his attempts to leave it.

The school too has its methods of labeling. Let us assume that a lower-class child, because of the inherent difficulty in meeting specific demands of the middle-class school, is in some conflict with his teachers. Let us further assume that the teacher wants a quiet classroom, and that the lower-class child, if Reissman[10] is to be believed, has had little experience with quiet rooms and does not see the value in silence. Let us imgaine that the conflict between this child and teacher becomes sufficiently severe so that the teacher writes out a referral notice and sends the child to the office. All referral notices are kept in the child's cumulative folder. At this point, the child is still an occasional deviant (the number of secondary deviants on the elementary level is very small—The entire Los Angeles City School System expelled only 600 children of elementary school age during the year 1960–1961).[11] The teacher, however, engages in what Goffman[12] calls *looping*, that is, the child's behavior in her class is discussed with other teachers over coffee so that when the child encounters these other teachers, his reputation has preceded him. At this point, he becomes a primary deviant, that is, the teachers consider him to be a potential "bad boy." From this point on, his behavior is under close scrutiny and even innocent acts may be considered deviant because they are defined by the teacher as such. Through this process, his cumulative folder becomes enlarged with referral notices until he is fully labeled and any nondeviant act is considered phony. If the child accepts the label of "bad boy," then he becomes a career or secondary deviant, thereby proving to the earlier teachers that they were right in pointing him out as a potential "bad boy." It is interesting to speculate on Fitzsimmons'[13] comment that teachers were able to predict juvenile delinquency in their students. It might be possible that they were able to label discipline problems in their class and then begin the process of causing the child to become a secondary deviant, thereby achieving a self-fulfilling prophecy.

Through the process of labeling, then, the school can aid in the process of neutralization, preparation, and desperation. It is likely to have a larger role in making lower-class delinquents than middle-class delinquents since the school has a predominantly middle-class orientation. It also tends to label boys as more prone to deviance than girls, since the school is a predominantly feminine-oriented institution and defines infractions from this standpoint.

If the lower-class child has a different attitude toward education than does the school, and if we assume that the school is in the power position and will punish lower-class behavior, we should be able to hypothesize that the lower-class child will have a lower self-image than would the children of the other classes.

Also, the lower-class student has a lower self-image with regard to the school. As pointed out by Montague,[14] there was a significant difference in the amount of satisfaction with the schools among status groups: the lower group was least satisfied and the middle group was most satisfied. The lower-status students seemed to suffer significantly from a feeling that they had difficulties with interpersonal relationships in school. Differences in difficulties with self-expression were significant at the 0.01 level, with the lower class again having the greatest difficulty. In the area of self-criticism, the lower-class student again showed a striking difference from the other two classes.

The general impression is that the lower-class student does not have advantages when he enters school and the pattern of disadvantage increases the longer he remains in school. The evidence would seem to indicate that the lower-class student has a negative self-image of himself while in school. When this is combined with Ausubel's[15] hypothesis that the lower-class child's academic and disciplinary misadventures lead to added frustration and thereby hostility, it is possible to postulate a connection between school misbehavior and juvenile delinquency: patterns learned in the school with regard to authority are simply carried over into the nonschool realm.

Discrimination in the School

Part of the problem of labeling and self-image in the schools is that both teachers and the institution as a whole are discriminatory. This is not to say that the school consciously practices prejudice. Although the process is often completely unintentional, it is nonetheless damaging. Here the problem is not so much neutralization as it is desperation. The feeling that fate rules the potential delinquent's life is increased through the covert and overt practice of discrimination. The first thing which a lower-class child notices is that there is a great teacher turnover. This teacher turnover dissuades the student from establishing any close ties with the teacher, even assuming that the school would allow close ties (one of the unwritten rules in most districts is that the teacher should not get too close to his students). The constant turnover, aside from affecting the educational process, also gives the child the feeling that his teachers really have no interest in him since they constantly leave him.[16] However, this is not the most serious problem with regard to building a feeling of desperation. The overt discrimination which is practiced in the school gives the child the feeling that no matter how hard he tries, nothing will come of it. He sees that the school discriminates against him, against his parents, and against his future.

There is no need to document at length the various overt forms of discrimination, but a brief listing is necessary in order to give some feeling for the pervasiveness of the problem; the reading texts used in the classrooms which typically contain material far less attuned to the interests of the disadvantaged; the Parent-Teacher Associations which often patronize or ignore underprivileged parents; the intelligence tests, the applicability of which to lower socio-economic groups is increasingly being questioned; the school psychologists and guidance counselors who frequently underestimate the possibility of the economically underprivileged child attending college; the friendship cliques and clubs which favor less the child from a poor neighborhood; the teacher's unfavorable images and expectations which militate against the respect and encouragement so needed by the child.[17]

This situation may actually cause more harm in an integrated school, for here the stigmatized child would more clearly see the difference between the treatment given his group and that given other groups. The black population of the school was used as an example in Chapter 11. The discriminatory practices of the school, however, can be focused upon any stigmatized group. It is true that the visibility of black and Mexican students makes their problems more difficult, but the school discriminates against the lower-class child in general. All this contributes to his desperation.

Our Schools Make Criminals

One systematic study of the school's role in making delinquents out of juveniles is a 1942 study by Arthur Johnson.[18] In this study, Johnson interviewed inmates in reform schools and prisons. Most of the responses he received could just as easily have been given by a present-day, lower-class child. In *Street Corner Research*,[19] for example, the general impression is that the school, when it is mentioned, is a hateful place which lowered the self-image and increased the feeling of fate of the lower-class child. The interviewing material collected by Johnson is equally enlightening.

The teacher tried to make me wear better clothes like the other children. I finally told her to go to hell and walked out. I swore then that I would have better clothes if I had to steal them and I did.

I had a stutter. I was put in a class with a lot of screwballs. My pals kidded me and I quit.

My mother was going nuts and I was worried about her. One day the teacher called me crazy too. I never went to school regular after that.

I was fired from school because I wouldn't study my history. When they brought me back and tried to make me study history again, I started to skip school.

I don't know why I ran away from school. I couldn't get along in a crowd, that's all.

I was put in a class with a lot of dumb clucks. It was too much for me and I quit.

One day I got to school late and was told that if I couldn't get there on time, not to come at all, just to spoil the class record. I took them at their word.[20]

Recommendations

Concrete steps can be taken by the schools in order to minimize the effects of neutralization, drift, and desperation. We suggest the following.

1. The school must recognize and appreciate the values of any deviant group, whether it be lower-class black, upper-class Oriental, or any other minority group.
2. In order to do this, the school must first investigate its own value biases on the basis of the behavior of the educational practitioners.
3. Labeling must cease. Cumulative folders, referral notices, and other such records must be put only to the use for which they were originally intended: to give teachers objective anecdotal and test information about students. These records should be used only by those teachers and counselors who have a direct relationship with the student. They are not designed nor should they ever be used as a depository of information for the business community, the police, or any other nonschool organization.
4. Discriminatory practices should be pointed out to the school, so that they can be eliminated.

The purpose of this chapter is not to present answers to specific problems, but rather to begin the theoretical formulation of possible future research on the school's role in juvenile delinquency. If the school is to serve a function in the treatment and prevention of delinquency, certain attitudes first must be changed on the part of the school. It is our contention that often it is not the child who is at fault, but rather that in his deviant behavior he is raising significant issues for the school.

NOTES

1. David Matza, *Delinquency and Drift*, Wiley, New York, 1964.
2. Albert K. Cohen, *Delinquent Boys: The Culture of the Gang*, Free Press, New York, 1955.

3. Richard Carlson, "Variations and Myth in the Social Status of Teachers," *Journal of Educational Sociology*, vol. 35, November, 1951, pp. 104–118.
4. L. A. Doyle, "Convergence and Divergence in Role Expectations of Elementary Teachers," *College of Education Quarterly*, winter, 1958, pp. 3–9.
5. Wilbur B. Brookover, and David Gottlieb, *A Sociology of Education*, American Book, New York, 1964.
6. Matza, *op. cit.*
7. Jules Henry, *Culture Against Man*, Random House, New York, 1963.
8. Fred J. Schanley, E. Longsteth Langdon, D. Welty Lefever, and Goven Olhagen. "Evaluation of a Special Program for Potential Dropouts," *Youth Studies Center*, University of Southern California, Los Angeles, 1961.
9. Thomas J. Scheff, "The Role of the Mentally Ill and the Dynamics of Mental Disorder: A Research Framework," *Sociometry*, vol. 26, no. 4, December, 1963.
10. Frank Riessman, *The Culturally Deprived Child.* Harper & Row, New York, 1962.
11. Dorothy F. Lyons and Virginia Powers, "Follow-Up Study of Elementary School Children Exempted from Los Angeles City Schools During 1960–1961," *Exceptional Children*, 1963.
12. Erwin Goffman. *Asylums*, Anchor Books, Doubleday, Garden City, N.Y., 1961.
13. Marion J. Fitzsimmons, "The Predictive Value of Teachers' Referrals," in Krugman, ed., *Orthopsychiatry and the School*, American Orthopsychiatric Association, New York, 1958.
14. Joel B. Montague, "Social Status and Adjustment in School," *The Clearing House*, vol. 27, September, 1952, pp. 19–24.
15. David P. Ausubel, "How Reversible are the Cognitive and Motivational Effects of Cultural Deprivation? Implications for Teaching the Culturally Deprived Child," *Urban Education*, vol. 1, Summer, 1964.
16. Riessman, *op. cit.*
17. Ralph Schwitzgebel, *Street Corner Research*, Harvard University Press, Cambridge, Mass., 1964.
18. Arthur C. Johnson, Jr., "Our Schools Make Criminals," *Journal of Criminal Law and Criminology*, vol. 33, November–December, 1942, pp. 310–315.
19. Schwitzgebel, *op. cit.*
20. Johnson, *op. cit.*

Chapter 15 / *The School and Mental Health*

This chapter considers the school's role in mental health as it relates to the creation of student careers within the school. Chapter 14 dealt with aspects of deviant student action which are negatively sanctioned by the school. Much of the deviant behavior discussed there would be considered criminal if the behavior were performed by an adult. This chapter also deals with deviant behavior, but not so much behavior which is negatively sanctioned or potentially criminal as behavior which is considered inappropriate and which the school attempts to change.

When working with potential delinquents, the school assumes that the student is responsible for his behavior, knows both what he is doing and why he does it, and can therefore be punished for it. When treating mental disorders, however, the school feels that even though the behavior may be just as bad, the student cannot always be held responsible for his behavior and therefore should not always be punished for it. The distinction between these two categories is somewhat fluid and to some extent depends upon the philosophy and the attitude of the school district. If the school district is psychologically oriented, it will tend to feel that much of the negative behavior is the result of a psychological problem. Should the school be more traditionally oriented, however, the identical behavior might be considered deviant, and punishment rather than therapy would be considered appropriate.

This chapter is divided into three basic sections. The first deals with the existentialist definition of mental health and mental illness and is based largely on the work of Viktor Frankl. The second section deals with the school's definition of mental health and shows the disparity between the definitions presented by Frankl and the operant definitions of the school. The third section is a summary and includes a short description of the conflict inherent in the difference between Frankl's and the school's definition of mental health.

Mental Health in the Twentieth Century

As has been the case in many of the preceding chapters, the single most difficult problem of this discussion is that of definition. For many years it was assumed that mental health and mental disorder could be defined in specific terms such as *schizophrenia* or *paronoia.* During the last decade, however, it has become clear to many writers that the categorical definitions of mental health and mental illness do not suffice as a model for analysis within complex institutions. One of the primary reasons for this is that each institution, each society, and each culture defines mental health in a different way.

For example, a person in our culture who holds a grudge for a period of 20 years and assumes that everyone else does likewise would be considered at least paranoiac. In many primitive tribes, however, a person who does not hold a grudge for 20 years, and who does not expect others to hold a grudge against him, is liable to find himself incapable of dealing with his society since he will be constantly attacked for slights and injustices which he has forgotten in the passage of time. Categorical definitions of mental health are more feasible in periods when intercultural contact is less common than it is now.

Of equal significance is the difference in definitions between various periods in the same culture. Frankl points out in his discussion of logotherapy that the definition of neurosis as presented by Freud or Adler at the beginning of the twentieth century is no longer feasible. He points out that Freud's definition of neurosis was largely societally determined (as are our own) and that Freud's time was most concerned with the breakdown of the Victorian ethic. This breakdown had its most obvious manifestations in sexual problems of one sort or another, and Freud's psychoanalysis was based largely upon this overt manifestation of a societal breakdown.

Adler, who wrote 15 years later (immediately before and after World War I), found that the basic problem facing patients was a feeling of inferiority, powerlessness, or perhaps, superiority. This again reflects the difficulties of a particular age, since the feeling of powerlessness was one of the characteristics of the period in which Adler did his most significant writing and speaking. Different ages and cultures manifest different psychological problems based upon the psychological and sociopsychological thought then prevalent.

There is a growing feeling among authors from a variety of fields that the neurosis of the present age cannot be discussed in the traditional terms of dynamisms or defense mechanisms, but rather must be defined and discussed in terms of the interrelationship of an individual with the society and how the individual finds *meaning* in that relationship.

Paul Goodman,[1] Jules Henry,[2] David Matza,[3] and Ralph Schwitzgebel[4] have all touched upon this problem. Systematic discussions of this construct appear in Frankl's *From Death Camp to Existentialism*[5] and Redl and Wineman's *Children Who Hate.*[6]

Frankl's discussion of the definition of mental health has four basic hypotheses. First, much of the behavior which a society might consider bizarre, neurotic, or even psychotic is not necessarily any of these. In the desire and the search for meaning within existence, the searcher may behave in a bizarre or ludicrous fashion. For example, there is reason to believe that the Bohemians of 40 years ago, the Beatniks of 10 to 15 years ago, and the civil rights marchers of 10 years ago were all expressing their feelings of a meaninglessness within the present society and in their own way were attempting to find a new meaning for their existence. The same can be said for today's hippies. Their behavior, style of dress, and mode of life might be considered bizarre, neurotic, or psychotic; but Frankl, Friedenberg, and Goodman all indicate that this seemingly bizarre behavior is actually an attempt both to point out to society that it is meaningless, and at the same time to build meaning within the individual.

Frankl does not necessarily agree with what they do, but he recognizes their behavior as an attempt to find meaning. His basic point is that whereas this behavior would have been considered neurotic or psychotic in a Freudian or Adlerian culture, it is by no means any of these things in the modern sense. It is a healthy search for meaning. As a corollary, Frankl points out that even if behavior is psychotic, this does not mean that it necessarily is wrong. As he comments, "Two and two also makes four when a paranoiac says so."

In connection with his first hypothesis, Frankl indicates that because of our tradition of adjustment psychiatry, we tend to equate suffering with mental illness and happiness with mental health. There is no reason to assume that the person who suffers is necessarily mentally ill. His suffering may be a sign of mental health in that he is searching for meaning in a society which he feels needs change. He suffers with the society and attempts to change it.

Frankl's second hypothesis deals with the genesis of existential frustration. He asks what the reaction will be if a person cannot find meaning in his existence. What if he is frustrated in this "most human demand"? Frankl postulates, as do Paul Tillich, Jean Paul Sartre, and Albert Camus, that this frustration is the basic condition of man. It is the *existential predicament*, and any thinking person who understands his situation will, of course, be frustrated. If the frustration reaches the point where the individual no longer feels capable of dealing with his society and with his frustrations, where he loses all sense of hope and direction, then he is caught by the modern existential neurosis. This leads us directly to Frankl's third hypothesis.

The third hypothesis relates to the distinction between existential frustration and *noogenic neurosis*. As Frankl has pointed out, existential frustration is not neurotic or psychotic. It is rather the predicament of the thoughtful man who is searching for meaning in his life. It is possible, however, for this existential frustration to lead to neurotic illness, that is, to noogenic neurosis. Frankl indicates that even in this case the noogenic neurosis is not caused by trauma in early childhood but rather is an outgrowth of the frustration and lack of meaning in the individual's life. It is an extension of existential frustration to the point where the individual has lost all feeling of purpose, all feeling of meaning, and is totally alienated from himself and from his society. In Frankl's terms, "noogenic neuroses have their roots not in psychological complexes and traumata but in spiritual problems and moral conflicts."

Frankl's fourth hypothesis deals with what he feels must be done for the man suffering from noogenic neurosis. He believes that the therapist must increase the individual's ability to deal meaningfully with his existence and must help him to find achievable goals and means by which to arrive at those goals. It is the purpose of the therapist, then, not so much to cure neurosis as it is to help the patient achieve a sense of meaningful homeostasis within his society. Thus, "The first and foremost aim of mental hygiene should be to stimulate man's will to meaning and to offer him concrete mental potentialities."

THE SCHOOL'S ROLE WITHIN THE EXISTENTIALIST SEARCH FOR MEANING

In relating Frankl's paradigm to the school's role in mental health, the following should be taken into consideration:

1. The basic mental health problem of the modern age is not one of the traditional neuroses or psychoses, but rather is one of a lack of meaning in the life of the student.
2. Those students who are most seriously searching for meaning in their existence may exhibit behaviors which by traditional

definitions would be considered at least neurotic and bizarre and possibly psychotic. Some acting out of overt behavior may in actuality be an attempt to determine the meaning of life.

3. There is no necessary relationship between adjustment and mental health. As a matter of fact, the "unadjusted" individual may be showing overt signs of mental health in that he is searching for meaning within the existential predicament of frustration.
4. The school's role, if it wishes to create mental health, must be that of aiding the student in the establishment of meaningful but attainable goals and of meaningful and possible means of arriving at those goals.

As Friedenberg[7] has stated, the school has two basic functions: (1) the clarification of experience, helping the student to know himself realistically and his society; and (2) the establishment of self-esteem, helping the student to accept himself.

The School's Definition of Mental Health

EVENTS LEADING TO PSYCHIATRIC CARE

Before beginning a discussion of how the school currently defines mental health, we need to know how an actor in any institution is led to psychiatric care. What is the sequence of events leading to the actor's being placed in the care of a therapist? Hollingshead and Redlich[8] suggest a four-point model for this sequence of events.

1. *The occurrence of abnormal behavior*, that is, actions which are different from what is expected in a social situation.[9] As was pointed out previously, the occurrence of deviant behavior is dependent upon the degree of similarity in the definition of proper behavior as seen by the individual and as seen by the institution. In the school situation, if the student and the school define a problem behavior in the same way, the probability of deviance being recognized is lessened. If the student defines deviance in a different way from the school,

however, then the probability of recognized occurrence of bizarre behavior is quite great.

2. *The appraisal of abnormal behavior.* Because the range of behavior is very great, the delimitation of that range depends upon an appraisal which is both interpersonal (how the institution views the disturbed person) and intrapersonal (how the disturbed person views himself).[10] If the individual is not willing to accept the interpersonal appraisal of the institution and he can convince a sufficient number of his peers of the inappropriateness of the institutional definition, then he can change it. It is, therefore, necessary that the institution's appraisal of the individual take into account not only its own desires but also the desires of the actors within the institution.

3. *The decision.* It is determined that psychiatric treatment is needed. This step is influenced by ". . . the assumed danger the behavior has for the disturbed person as well as for those around him; the attitude of friends and family toward treatment; and the availability of treatment." The basic difficulty is that whereas extreme clinical categories are often recognized, the residual categories may not be recognized as needing psychiatric care.

4. *Implementation of the decision.* This may not always be possible, since help may not be available.

The appraisal system outlined above is the basis of Hollingshead and Redlich's model. The biases of the school to be discussed are central to the school's appraisal of deviant or disturbed behavior. The school has both a middle-class bias and a bias against overt behavior, and consequently it tends to define deviance within this framework. For instance, the lower-class, overt nonacademic child may be defined as deviant simply because he disturbs the class and does not get his work done.

The process may end here, for the school often has neither the facilities nor, in many cases, the desire to implement psychiatric care. Most often the child is merely appraised or labeled as deviant or disturbed and is dealt with within the school structure. The process is something akin to the following:

1. The child behaves in an eccentric fashion.
2. The teacher takes note of the behavior but attempts to handle the problem in the classroom.
3. If the problem continues and passes the teacher's tolerance level, a referral notice will be sent to the counselor or principal (teachers are not encouraged to handle "serious" behavioral problems in the classroom).
4. The labeling process has begun in earnest since the child is now labeled by both the teacher and the school as a *problem*, a *potential deviant*, or a *disturbed child*, depending on the philosophy of the school (The child who is a *deviant* in one school may be classified as mentally disturbed in the next).
5. Once the child is labeled, the looping process, both in its formal and its informal aspects, begins.
6. The child passes on to the next teacher as a recognized potential deviant. Because of this, the tolerance limit of the new teacher is far lower than that of the teacher who had the child as a nondeviant.
7. The child has a greater tendency to get into trouble since behavior which might be innocent is defined within the scope of the deviant label which the school has applied. This in turn increases the conflict.
8. Somewhere within this process, the child may come to believe what the school has said about him. At this point the child becomes a career deviant.

The single most important aspect of this process is *appraisal*, and it is therefore necessary to analyze the biases of the school which affect the appraisal and the definition of mental health. There are three specific perspectives within the school which significantly affect this appraisal: (1) the school's middle-class orientation, (2) the philosophy of the school, and (3) the school's attitude toward overt behavior.

THE SCHOOL'S MIDDLE-CLASS ORIENTATION

Though teachers may come from all social classes,[11] their orientation as teachers tends to be consistent with the middle-class. Doyle[12] and Brookover[13] give excellent examples of middle-class orientation and behavior among teachers. The attitudes which they cite are those with which the school is expected, by parents and the community, to imbue the student.

One of the difficulties with this middle-class orientation in the school is that some of the patterns which the school considers middle class are actually outdated and at variance with the rest of the society. For example, the school teaches that the child should be honest in all things. It also teaches the value of the government and the importance of supporting that government, both through the bearing of arms and the paying of taxes. The latter is particularly of interest since the tax laws of the United States have built-in loopholes so that no one will have to pay the full tax officially listed. If the upper socio-economic classes were to pay the taxes for which they are originally slated, there would be little or no money left for reinvestment or saving. If the taxpayer were to take the teachings of the school literally, he would find himself in the peculiar situation of paying more taxes than the government had expected him to pay, and he soon would find himself bankrupt. Thus the ideal values presented to the young student are at variance with the operant values of the society in general.

It would be irrelevant to debate whether the values of the school or those of society are of intrinsically greater worth. The point here is, that not only does the middle-class bias of the school operate to a detriment of the lower-class child, but it may also operate to a detriment of the middle-class child. This class bias will have a direct effect on the school's definition and appraisal of deviant or disturbed behavior, since the child will often be operating from his own particular class bias, while the school will be acting according to its ideal middle-class values. In short, conflict can be expected on any class level since the culture or "related meanings and values" would be different for the institution and for any of its students.

THE PHILOSOPHY OF THE SCHOOL

The educational principles of the school will have an effect upon the definition and appraisal of deviance. If, for instance, the school has a progressive philosophy, there will be great emphasis upon individual, social, and psychological as well as mental growth. There will be a tendency to accept more overt behavior: more discussion among the students as they solve a group problem, walking around the room, singing, and so forth. In this atmosphere, the preschizophrenic child will be appraised as disturbed or at least deviant since "he is withdrawn and uncooperative." The child who acts out, so long as the acting does not become extreme, will be valued as "a creative, contributing member of the group."

On the other hand, if the school is primarily interested in academic pursuits, then the definition of deviance may well be reversed. If, for example, the lecture method is used, acting out, talking, and moving about may be defined as hyperkinetic behavior, while the quiet child who says nothing but turns in at least a minimum of work will be considered a good citizen. Schizophrenic behavior might actually be reinforced by giving the quiet child high grades in cooperation, and thereby strengthening his belief that his behavior is acceptable.

It should be noted that there has been an apparent shift in emphasis from student as problem solver (and therefore overt in his behavior) which characterized the Progressive Education Association Projects of the 1930s and 1940s to the student as learner of specific knowledge (and therefore quiet) as characterized by the Basic Education Association Reports. The emphasis on specific knowledge has been heightened since education has become part of the national defense system wherein an educated population is necessitated by highly technical and complex defense mechanisms. Accordingly, the effect of this emphasis upon the definition and appraisal of disturbance and student deviance should be noted.

THE SCHOOL'S ATTITUDE TOWARD OVERT BEHAVIOR

On the school level, discipline problems are defined in terms of overt behavior—usually a lack of decorum. That is, schools tend to equate a lack of decorum with disturbed or deviant behavior. For example, Hayes has compiled a list of behaviors which teachers find objectionable by asking teachers to list behaviors which "were a definite interference to learning in the classroom."

1. Whispering (against class usage, creating a disturbance)
2. Paying attention to another student instead of to the work at hand
3. Unnecessary noise, hitting pencil on desk, dropping books, etc.
4. Talking aloud (against class usage, creating a disturbance)
5. Laughing so as to disturb others, making queer noises, whistling.
6. Moving without permission, wandering around
7. "Wisecrack," asking questions, making silly remarks
8. Direct disobedience to authority (for example, refusing to move when told) . . .

23. Refusal to answer, obvious withdrawal[14]

Item 23 is included because it is the only one on the list which is not some form of overt acting out.

Many of the behavioral characteristics which the school regards as serious would not be considered so by clinicians. Wickman's early study[15] indicates the difference between the ratings of teachers and mental hygienists. His study was repeated by Mitchell[16] in 1940 The findings are as follows:

RANKING OF BEHAVIORS CONSIDERED MOST SERIOUS BY TEACHERS AND MENTAL HYGIENISTS IN 1927 (WICKMAN) AND 1940 (MITCHELL)

Offense	TEACHERS 1940	TEACHERS 1927	HYGIENISTS 1940	HYGIENISTS 1927
Heterosexual offenses	1	1.0	20	25.0
Stealing	2	2.0	5	13.5
Obscene notes	3	3.0	25	28.5
Cruelty	4	8.0	3	6.0
Untruthfulness	5	5.0	15	24.0
Masturbation	6	3.0	35	40.0
Lack of sociability	7	39.5	1	1.0
Destructiveness	8	10.0	22	44.0
Fearfulness	9	36.0	4	5.0
Cheating	10	9.0	16	23.0
Truancy	16	6.0	24	23.0
Defiance and impertinence	21	7.0	35	36.5

This divergence between the ratings of teachers and mental hygienists has serious consequences for both occurrence and appraisal, since many children who are disturbed may never be noticed whereas many deviant children may be labeled disturbed. Both Wickman and Mitchell believed that the problem lay in the teacher's middle-class behavioral norms: neatness, punctuality, politeness, quietness, and so forth. Specifically, Wickman felt that the things which disturbed teachers most were those student activities which directly attacked the teacher's authority or prestige in the classroom. Clark[17] later found that either Wickman was wrong or that there had been a change in attitude, since teachers now felt that those activities which disturbed the classroom's learning atmosphere were most serious. Furthermore, in Clark's study there was some closing of the gap between the appraisals of the teachers and hygienists. The behavior which bothered teachers most, however, was still the most overt behavior: lying, tattling, picking on younger children, and so forth.

Lyons and Powers[18] point out ten activities listed by teachers as reasons for recommending exemption or expulsion.

1. Emotional instability
2. Hyperkinetic behavior syndrome
3. Antisocial behavior
4. Aggressive, abnormal behavior
5. Psychosis and neurosis
6. Personality disorder
7. Immaturity
8. Emotional disturbance
9. Hyperactive acting out
10. Emotional disturbance associated with mental retardation

It can be seen that most of the categories are of an overt nature or are normally defined as such by teachers. For example, immaturity is defined as, "can't sit still, noisy, bothers others."

It can be seen that the school has a definite bias against overt acting-out behavior. Under these circumstances mental health would again necessarily be defined in terms of this particular bias; the acting-out child would be more liable to the labeling process than would the reticent, quiet child, and many deviant children could be defined as disturbed.

Of even greater import than that some deviant children will be defined as disturbed is that many children who are disturbed will not be recognized as such by the school. Since the school's particular bias is against overt behavior, the child who is not overt in his disturbance will very often be ignored. For example, if a teacher has 40 students and the class tends to be boisterous, it may be difficult, if not impossible for her to recognize the problems of the quiet child who sits in the back of the room and does a minimal amount of work. This is not to say that the child is necessarily schizophrenic, but only that if the child were schizophrenic the possibility exists that the teacher would not recognize him as such. In the first place, withdrawn autistic behavior is not so easily recognizable as the overt acting-out behavior and, second, the philosophy of the school would tend toward making the teacher ignore withdrawn behavior and respond to acting-out behavior.

Summary

The first section of this chapter attempted to define mental health in a way which has meaning for the present existential situation of the school and its students. The second section dealt largely with the way in which the school actually defines problems of mental health. It is obvious that there is very little correlation between these two points of view. Whereas Frankl, Goodman, Friedenberg, and others speak in terms of the importance of meaning and the importance of value and honor within the life of the student, the school tends to speak in terms of the somewhat archaic middle-class constructs of quietness, decorum, adjustment, and propriety.

While Frankl, Goodman, Friedenberg, and others would say that the most creative and deepest thinkers among students are those who ask the embarrassing questions, who do act out, and who often cause us a great deal of trouble in the school, the school speaks of its most creative and honored students as those who are in academically advanced programs, who get to school on time, and whose attendance and citizenship are above reproach. If it is true that the neuroses and psychoses of mid-twentieth-century America are those of meaning, insight, and honor, then there is not merely an option but an imperative that the school encourage the embarrassing questions and give students greater authority and responsibility for their own behaviors—both academic and social. If Frankl, Redl, Friedenberg, Goodman, Henry, and the other social critics are correct —and we believe they are—the school must learn to recognize students as discrete individuals whose problems, ideas, and behaviors must be seen from their perspective as well as the perspective of the teacher.

NOTES

1. Paul Goodman, *Growing Up Absurd*, Random House, New York 1956.
2. Jules Henry, *Culture Against Man*, Random House, New York, 1963.
3. David Matza, *Delinquency and Drift*, Wiley, New York, 1964.
4. Ralph Schwitzgebel, *Street Corner Research*, Harvard University Press, Cambridge, Mass., 1964.
5. Viktor Frankl, *From Death Camp to Existentialism*, Beacon Press, Boston, 1959.
6. Fritz Redl and David Wineman, *Children Who Hate*, Free Press, New York, 1951.
7. Edgar Z. Friedenberg, *The Vanishing Adolescent*, Dell, New York, 1959.
8. August B. Hollingshead and Frederick C. Redlich, *Social Class and Mental Illness*, Wiley, New York, 1958.
9. Goodman, *op. cit.*
10. Henry, *op. cit.*
11. Richard C. Carlson, "Variations and Myth in the Social Status of Teachers," *Journal of Educational Sociology*, vol. 35, November, 1951, pp. 104–118.
12. L. A. Doyle, "Convergence and Divergence in Role Expectations of Elementary Teachers," *College of Education Quarterly*, winter, 1958, pp. 3–9.

13. Wilbur Brookover and David Gottlieb, *A Sociology of Education*, American Book, New York, 1964.
14. Margret L. Hayes, "A Study in Classroom Disturbances of Eighth Grade Boys and Girls," *Teachers College, Contributions to Education*, no. 871, Columbia University Press, New York, 1943, p. 20.
15. E. K. Wickman, "Children's Behavior and Teachers' Attitudes," The Commonwealth Fund, New York, 1928.
16. J. C. Mitchell, "A Study of Teachers' and Mental Hygienists' Ratings of Certain Behavior Problems of Children," *Journal of Educational Research*, vol. 36, 1943, pp. 297–307.
17. Elmer J. Clark, "Teacher's Reactions Toward Objectionable Pupil Behavior," *Elementary School Journal*, April, 1951, pp. 446–449.
18. Dorothy F. Lyons and Virginia Powers, "Follow-Up Study of Elementary School Children Exempted from Los Angeles City Schools During 1960–61," *Exceptional Children*, December, 1963.